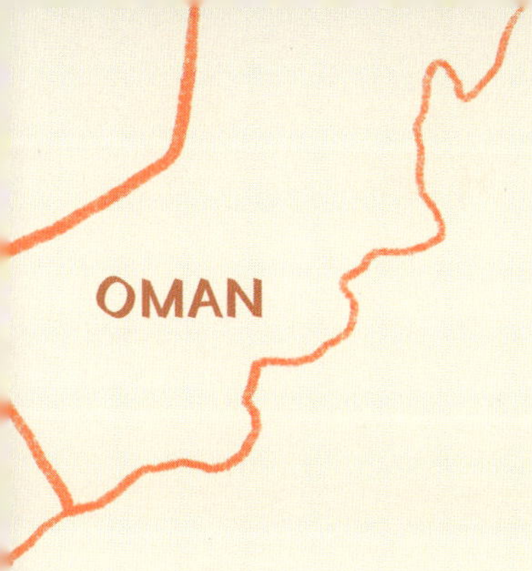
OMAN

Enebla
እንብላ

Enebla

እንብላ

Recipes from an Ethiopian Kitchen

LULADEY MOGES

TOUCHWOOD

For more information, contact the publisher at:

TouchWood Editions
touchwoodeditions.com

Edited by Lesley Cameron
Cover and interior design by Tree Abraham
Family photos and ephemera are from the personal collections of the author and the designer.

CATALOGUING INFORMATION AVAILABLE FROM LIBRARY AND ARCHIVES CANADA
ISBN 9781771513623 (HARDCOVER)
ISBN 9781771513630 (E-BOOK)

TouchWood Editions acknowledges that the land on which we live and work is within the traditional territories of the Lkwungen (Esquimalt and Songhees), Malahat, Pacheedaht, Scia'new, T'Sou-ke and WSÁNEĆ (Pauquachin, Tsartlip, Tsawout, Tseycum) peoples.

We acknowledge the financial support of the Province of British Columbia through the Book Publishing Tax Credit.

BRITISH COLUMBIA

This book was produced using FSC®-certified, acid-free papers, processed chlorine free, and printed with soya-based inks.

Printed in China

26 25 24 23 22   1 2 3 4 5

This book is dedicated to my beautiful mother, Newaye Kidanu, who taught me most of the recipes in this book and has been my rock and guiding light all my life. And to my father, Moges Tilahun, who was the best person I have ever known. He fostered my love for food and taught me the importance of family. I am my mother's daughter and forever daddy's little girl.

"Go, eat your food with gladness and drink your wine with a joyful heart"
— Ecclesiastes 9:7

ሂድ፣ ምግብህን በደስታ ብላ፤ ልብህም ደስ ብሎት የወይን ጠጅህን ጠጣ፤+
እውነተኛው አምላክ በሥራህ ደስ ተሰኝቷልና።
— መክብብ 9:7

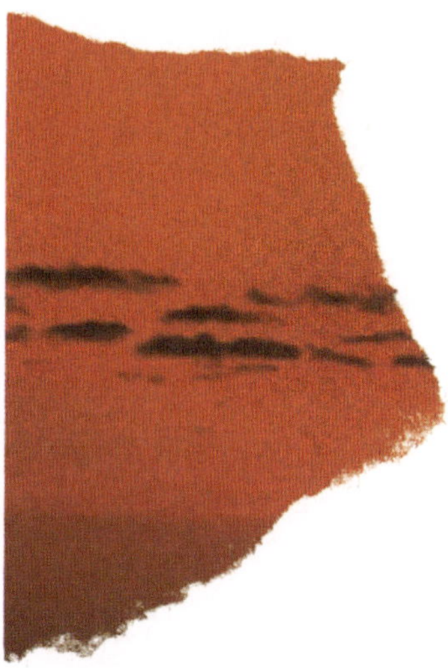

CONTENTS

12-4-51
PHOTO GEORGES
Cunningham Street No. 56
13 DEC 1958

INTRODUCTION

Ethiopia is located in the Horn of Africa. Rich in history, culture, and natural resources—Lucy, possibly the most famous fossil in the world, was discovered in the Hadar region and dates back three million years—it is one of only two nations in Africa that have never been colonized, despite several attempts by the Italians. Paleoanthropologists consider Ethiopia to be the epicenter of the cradle of humankind and civilization. It is also my birthplace.

I was born in Addis Ababa, the capital of Ethiopia, in the mid-1980s. My memories of my early childhood are filled with playing outside for hours in our garden with my siblings and our family dog, Benji. My dad was very into nature and gardening and had several plants, herbs, and trees like apples, coffee, limes, and tomatoes to list a few. My brother and I would always try to sneak an apple or a tomato without my father finding out, but he always managed to know—or to catch us in the act.

We were fortunate enough to have help at home. Once my schoolwork was done, I would sneak into the kitchen and watch the maids cook our meals. They prepared most of the meals in the second kitchen of the house, which was a place I was not allowed to go as a child. There were a lot of open flames, hot coals that were not always attended to, and the *mitad*, the very hot stove-top grill where the maids cooked the injera (page 129). As an adult, I understand why it was not a place for a child, but back then I found every excuse to sneak in to watch and learn. Those moments are where my love for food and cooking began.

My love of food and cooking was nurtured in other ways as well. I adored my family's weekend visits to my grandparents' house, where I would watch my grandmother and my auntie cook. I also had a chance to cook with my grandmother on those weekends, but my favorite thing of all was watching her make her special shiro wot (chickpea stew, page 69). But even though I watched her for hours and even learned her secret recipe, the reality is that I

could never make it like she did. (Neither could my mother or my aunties!) She had a special touch that none of us have been able to recreate but constantly strive to get close to.

Another fond childhood memory is of all the gatherings and parties my parents hosted. Every weekend was a celebration. From barbecues to mark the end of the week or simply bring our community together, to more elaborate celebrations such as birthday and anniversary parties, my parents used any excuse to have family and friends over.

These get-togethers always involved an abundance of food, with a variety of traditional and non-traditional selections. Some weekends we would have Italian or North American food selections, which were always a hit as they were something different and a treat. The menu would consist of meatballs, fried cauliflower, french fries, lasagna, skewers, spaghetti, burgers . . . My mother would oversee the menu planning and help the maids with the cooking. My aunts would come over to help with the cooking as well. I was sometimes allowed to help with the "easy" tasks of rolling meatballs or mixing batter—which meant the world to me.

Other times, we would have traditional Ethiopian food like kitfo (Ethiopian beef tartare, page 99), doro wot (spicy chicken stew, page 95), grilled fiyel (grilled goat), zilzil tibs (sautéed beef strips, page 113), and beg wot (lamb stew, page 109) were just some of the favorites we enjoyed regularly at these events. These dishes would be made by our maids, who understood my love of all things food-related and would sneak me into the kitchen when my mom was not looking. While I was careful to avoid getting cut or burned, one time I was chased and stomped on by a chicken.

It happened during the preparation for one of my parents' special events. I can't remember what the occasion was, but I do remember that we were having doro wot and I was seven years old. I had snuck into the kitchen as usual and was quietly watching and learning how to make this favorite dish when the house phone started ringing. Our maid Meseret ran off to the main house to answer the phone, leaving me unattended with the chicken. Once my unsupervised rival realized that we were alone, it took the opportunity to make a run for it. My young mind thought it wanted to attack me, so I took off running too—and the chase was on. We ran through the back of the house into the garden area. After what felt like a lifetime, everything came to an abrupt halt when I tripped over my shoelaces. At this point, my adversary only saw me as a speed bump and stomped all over me to get away. My child's mind was convinced that the chicken was after me and was going to hurt me, although it was simply trying not to be dinner. Needless to say, I am still scared of live chickens and, in fact, all birds.

For the most part, my family ate beef, chicken, or goat, but every Ethiopian holiday meal is based on a specific animal. Christmas dinner involves a sacrificial lamb, and Easter dinner always features a chicken, for example. And during Lent, we would eat only vegetarian or vegan dishes like shiro wot (chickpea stew, page 69), misir wot (lentil stew, page 67), and gomen wot (collard greens stew, page 79). Our culture is immersed in food, whether we are celebrating or commiserating. Food is at the center of all our gatherings, and it is one of the main focal points that shaped my childhood.

★

In the mid-1990s, Ethiopia was embroiled in a civil war that seemed unending. In a desire to find safety, a better life, and access to quality education, my parents made the life-changing decision to move us to the United States. Our first stop was Dallas, Texas. It was definitely a culture shock as well as an exciting adventure.

While we had been used to eating Western foods back home, I was not prepared for the abundance or variety that greeted us in Texas. So many fast foods to choose from, so many restaurants offering cuisines from all four corners of the world . . . My young culinary mind was intrigued by the endless possibilities to learn about new cooking techniques.

Our first trip to an American grocery store was to an Albertsons. The aisles and aisles of candy, chips, and sodas had me wondering if I was in heaven. My siblings and I were used to eating plain Kellogg's Corn Flakes, which were always a treat, and now here I was standing in a cereal aisle with more flavors and cereal options than I could ever have imagined. My brother and I were so overwhelmed by the choices that we agreed to just get Kellogg's because we at least knew what we were getting. Of course, over time, we found the confidence to experiment with other types of cereal, but to this day—call me sentimental—you will always find the exact same type of Kellogg's Corn Flakes that I enjoyed as a child in my kitchen cupboard.

My parents had a smooth transition to life in the States. Luckily, we had a lot of family and friends who lived in Dallas, which helped us get settled in. Dallas also has a large Ethiopian population, so there were several Ethiopian markets and restaurants where we could purchase spices and ingredients. For the most part, though, my mom or dad would bring back the main spices like berbere, shiro, and mitmita from Addis, when they went back to visit once or twice a year. These are staple ingredients that you will always find in any Ethiopian's freezer or pantry.

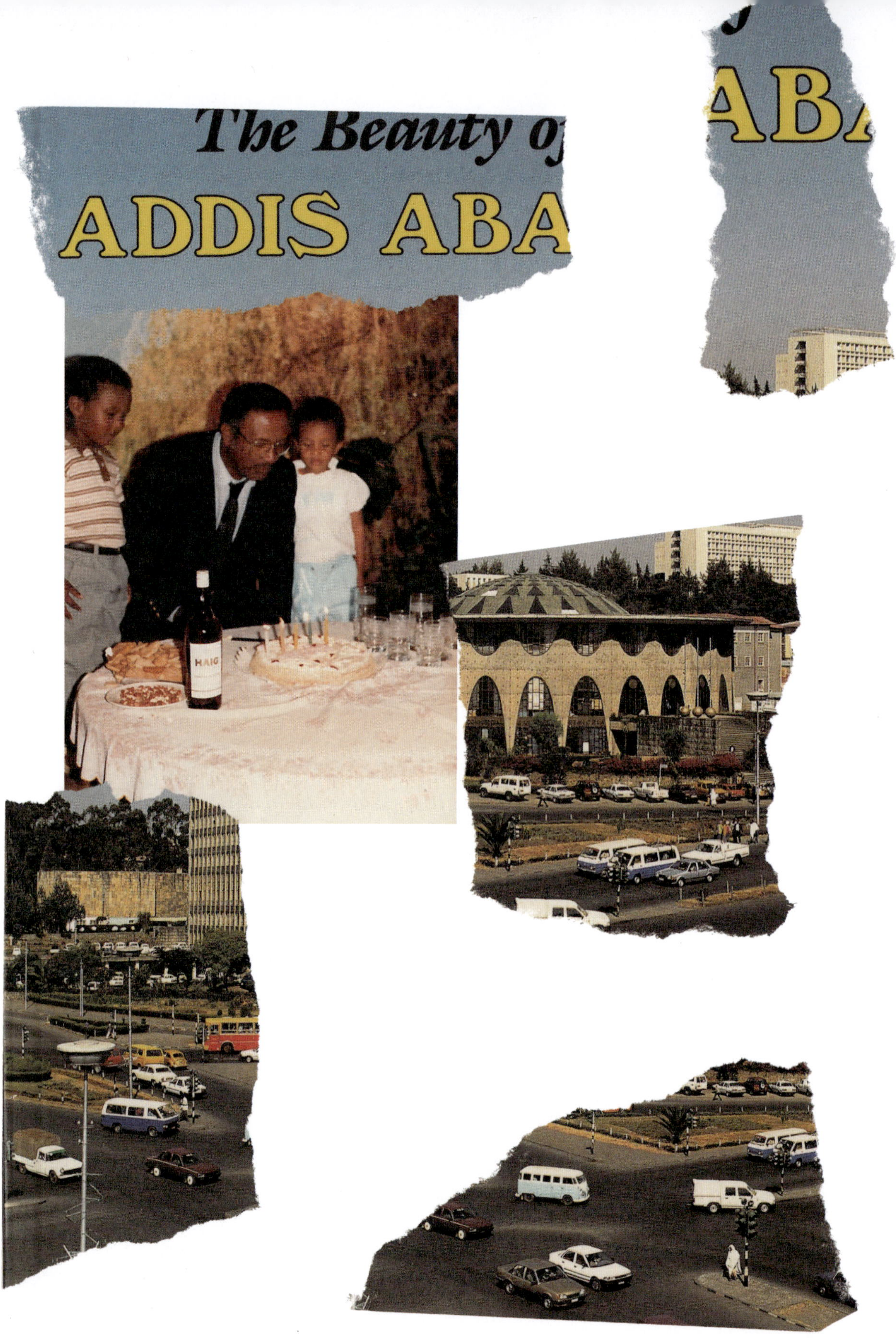
The Beauty
ADDIS ABA
ABA
HAIG

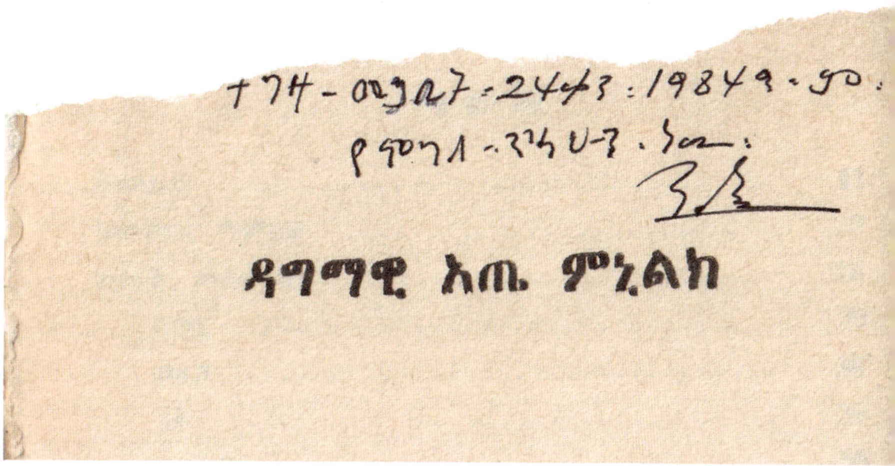

Aside from the culinary changes, one big difference for me was language. While my brother had learned English in his all-boys school in Addis, my sister and I attended Italian school, which meant we spoke only Italian and Amharic, our native language. The only English I knew was "My name is Lula," which made it quite difficult to assimilate and make friends. I had to attend ESL classes and tried my hardest to grasp the new culture and figure out my new "home." Our parents had a different struggle. They were trying to make sure that we did not forget where we came from and that we respected and honored our culture and history. Although my teenage self did not fully appreciate or understand their motives at the time, one of the things that I am very thankful for today is the very strict household rule my parents always maintained: "We might live in America, but once you come home, this is Ethiopia."

That meant we continued our tradition of family dinners every night and weekend gatherings with our extended family and friends. The main difference with the weekend gatherings was that we would now rotate them week by week between our house, my uncle's house, and my aunt's house, etc. At home, we no longer had maids to cook for us. Instead, my parents would take turns making our meals. My mother did most of the cooking, though, as my dad only had three or four "specialties." I was now allowed to help my mom in the kitchen more, which gave me an opportunity to continue learning how to make our traditional dishes.

I am forever grateful that my parents moved us to the United States. I know they had to sacrifice much that was dear to them to do so. I'm even more grateful that they taught us our Ethiopian culture, traditions, and cuisines even after we left our homeland. This journey helped me develop my love for cooking and sharing recipes and cemented my lovely memories of my childhood. All the recipes in this book have been taught to me by family and friends or passed down through my family. I am excited to share them with you and to introduce you to some Ethiopian culinary traditions along the way. I hope you love them the way I do.

CULTURE, YIELDS & INGREDIENTS

Culture

Enebla directly translates to "let's eat." As I mentioned earlier, our culture is very food-centric, so when you are eating and guests come over or you see another person, it is very common to start by saying "Enebla!" This is to invite them to join you and it is very standard etiquette.

Another very common practice related to eating together is literally feeding each other. This is called *gursha*, which translates directly to English as "mouthful." It is a cultural way of showing love, appreciation, friendship, and respect. While eating together, you would feed another person at the table—using either your hand or a spoon to put the food in their mouth—as an act of respect. The person who's been honored with the gursha then returns the favor.

Abesha (or Habesha) is a term used to identify people from Ethiopia and Eritrea. It refers to anyone who was born in, or is a descendant of someone who was born in, the land called Abyssinia in biblical times—present-day Ethiopia and Eritrea.

Religion plays a big role in the Ethiopian culture. The country is predominantly Christian with faiths like Ethiopian Orthodox, Pentay (a short form of Pentecostal, sometimes written as P'ent'ay), and Roman Catholic being prevalent. Other major religions are Islam and Judaism. This long historical connection between religion and culture is deeply rooted in Ethiopian society and is important in each person's day-to-day life and identity. As a religious sacrifice, each religion has a fasting period; the times vary based on the faith you follow. For example, people who are Ethiopian Orthodox fast seven times a year, including for Lent, 55 days prior to Easter (Catholics fast for 40 days for Lent). In addition to the seven fasting periods, they fast every Wednesday and Friday throughout the year. During fasting, people abstain from all animal products like meat, dairy, and eggs. These fasting times are why we have such a huge selection of vegetarian and vegan food options.

Yields

Given our traditional preference for eating in groups, it is very hard to make Ethiopian food for just one person, so most recipes in this book make four to six portions. Plus, the wots (stews) get better and improve their flavor after being left overnight, so they make great leftovers, which means there's no need to worry about making too much.

Ingredients

The ingredients in this book are a mix of traditional Ethiopian ingredients and ingredients you're probably very familiar with. For the Ethiopian ingredients, I highly recommend going to an Ethiopian market to buy them. If you have questions, the staff in the market will probably be able to help you out. Alternatively, you should be able to find most of the ingredients in African markets, Asian markets, or international food stores. If all else fails, most of the ingredients are also available online.

For substitution options, some recipes offer alternative options in the ingredients list (these are always listed after my recommended ingredient) but I do not recommend using other alternatives, as it will change the outcome of the finished product.

Kibe (Ethiopian butter) is one of the ingredients that I highly recommend purchasing at an Ethiopian market. If you cannot find it, use olive oil or vegetable oil as listed in the ingredients of each recipe, but do not use regular butter in place of kibe. Kibe (also known as niter kibbeh) is made by clarifying butter and infusing it with herbs and spices, including black pepper, turmeric, fenugreek seeds, and cumin to list only a few. It is similar to ghee and is not only used for cooking but is also traditionally used as a hair treatment.

Berbere is a fragrant red spice blend containing over 20 spices. With a blend of chilies and spices like fenugreek, cinnamon, cardamom, coriander, and nutmeg, to list a few, each household has their own version of this spice. Another popular spice is mitmita, which is made of hot peppers and spices. It is spicier than berbere, so it is mostly used as a condiment.

Tibs is a true staple in Ethiopian cuisine. It is meat that is sautéed or stir-fried. The meat is cut into small cubes and cooked with vegetables, herbs, and spices. Like most of our dishes, it is traditionally eaten with injera (page 129) and the most popular meats are beef, lamb, and goat. Tibs is very versatile and comes in several variations that depend on the meat used. When you say just "tibs," it means beef. For all other meats, the meat that is used in the dish will come first in the name of the dish. For example, if you want fish that is stir-fried, you would say asa tibs (fish stir-fry, page 115) or if it's goat that is stir-fried, you would say fiyel tibs (goat stir-fry). Ethiopians in general are huge meat lovers, and cooking it "tibs-style" has been standard over the centuries. It is a dish prepared as a sign of respect and takes center stage on the table at family gatherings and holiday celebrations. Another popular ways to serve beef is raw with a side of mitmita (page 99). If that is too much for you, tibs is the way to go. You'll find a selection of tibs recipes on pages 113–117.

Commonly used ingredients

Unless otherwise specified, salt is plain table salt or iodized salt, pepper is ground black pepper, oil is vegetable oil or olive oil (based on your preference), and sugar is granulated.

THE TACO BELL TEST

How can you measure something as personal as your reaction to spicy food? This was a problem I faced when, as a college student, I started cooking for my friends for the first time. Some of them (like me) loved their dishes hot, but some others just couldn't cope with spices at all. How was I to plan a menu under those circumstances? Help arrived from an unexpected quarter: Taco Bell. Familiar with this problem, they grade their sauces according to five strengths, Breakfast Salsa, Mild, Hot, Fire, and Diablo. So when you're menu planning, check in with your guests and find out how they take their tacos. Anyone who likes a Fire or Diablo sauce will enjoy a full-strength awaze tibs (page 114), for example. If you're cooking for a Mild or Hot audience, then dial down on the jalapeño peppers accordingly and make the derek tibs (page 114).

GLOSSARY

Here are the names of some traditional dishes and ingredients in Ethiopian food culture. I've given you their name in Amharic script and an English translation. You'll see that I've used the Amharic names of many of these ingredients in the recipes.

Not all of the recipe titles in this book have a formal English translation. Where there isn't a direct translation, I've given more of a description of the dish, so you'll see similar descriptions for recipe titles in a couple of spots.

Name	Amharic	English Translation
Abol	አቦል	First cup of Ethiopian coffee
Alicha	አልጫ	Mild stew
Alicha doro wot	የአልጫ ዶሮ ወጥ	Mild chicken stew
Alicha siga wot	የሰጋ አልጫ ወጥ	Mild beef stew
Ambasha	አምባሻ	Traditional bread
Asa	አሳ	Fish
Asa tibs	አሳ ጥብስ	Fried fish
Asa wot	የዓሣ ወጥ	Fish stew
Ater kik	አተር ክክ	Split pea
Atkilt	አትክልት	Vegetables
Atmit duket	አጥሚት	Oats and barley flour mixture
Atmit with bula	አጥሚት	Ethiopian porridge drink
Atmit with gebs	የገብስ አጥሚት	Ethiopian oats drink
Awaze	አዋዜ	Ethiopian hot sauce
Awaze tibs	አዋዜ ጥብስ	Extra spicy beef stir-fry
Ayib	አይብ	Ethiopian cheese
Azifa	አዚፋ	Ethiopian lentil salad
Baklava	ባቅላቫ	Baklava
Beef sambusa	የሰጋ ሳምቡሳ	Beef samosas
Beg	በግ	Lamb
Berbere	በርበሬ	Ethiopian blend of spices
Beso duket	የበሶ ዱቄት	Roasted barley blend
Bula	ቡላ	Ethiopian breakfast dish
Bula duket	ቡላ ዱቄት	False banana powder
Buna	ቡና	Coffee
Buticha	ቡጥጫ	Ethiopian chickpea dish

Chechebsa	ጨጨብሳ	Ethiopian breakfast dish
Chicken cotoletta	ኮቲሌቲ	Ethiopian chicken schnitzel
Chiko	ጭኮ	Ethiopian coffee snack
Dabo	ዳቦ	Bread
Dabo kolo	ዳቦ ቆሎ	Ethiopian little fried snack
Defo dabo	ድፎ ዳቦ	Ethiopian bread
Derek tibs	ደረቅ ጥብስ	Strips of beef stir-fry
Dinbilal	ድንብላል	Coriander
Dinich	ድንች	Potato
Doro	ዶሮ	Chicken
Doro tibs	ዶሮ ጥብስ	Chicken stir-fry
Doro wot	ዶሮ ወጥ	Spicy chicken stew
Duba	ዱባ	Pumpkin
Duba wot	የዱባ ወጥ	Pumpkin stew
Enqulal	እንቁላል	Eggs
Enqulal firfir	እንቁላል ፍርፍር	Ethiopian scrambled eggs
Erd	እርድ	Turmeric
Ergo	እርጎ	Ethiopian yogurt
Etan machesha	እጣን ማጨሻ	Incense burner for coffee ceremony
Firfir	ፍርፍር	Injera scrambled in stew
Fitfit	ፍትፍት	Injera tossed in stew
Fiyel	ፍየል	Goat
Fiyel tibs	የፍየል ጥብስ	Goat stir-fry
Fossolia	ፎሶሊያ	Ethiopian-style green beans
Ful	ፉል	Spicy Ethiopian fava beans
Genfo	ገንፎ	Ethiopian porridge
Gesho entchet	ጌሾ እንጨት	Hops stems
Gomen wot	ጎመን	Collard greens stew
Gomen be siga	ጎመን በስጋ	Collard greens with beef stew
Gored gored	ጎረድ ጎረድ	Cubed beef
Injera	እንጀራ	Ethiopian sour flatbread
Jebena	ጀበና	Ethiopian coffee pot
Karia	ቃሪያ	Pepper
Kategna	ቃተኛ	Ethiopian spicy flatbread
Key sir	ቀይ ስር	Ethiopian beets and potatoes
Kibe	ቅቤ	Ethiopian butter
Kinche	ቅንጨ	Cracked wheat/bulgur

Kitfo	ክትፎ	Ethiopian beef tartare
Kita	ቂጣ	Ethiopian spicy flatbread
Kochkocha	ቆጭቆጫ	Ethiopian jalapeño hot sauce
Korerima	ኮረሪማ	Cardamom
Kurs	ቁርስ	Breakfast
Kuti	ቁጢ	Ethiopian tea and coffee blend
Vegetarian lasagna	የአትክልት ላዛኛ	Vegetarian lasagna
Lasagna with meat	የስጋ ላዛኛ	Lasagna with meat
Mefcha	መፍጫ	Mortar and pestle
Mekoya	መቆያ	Snack
Milifoli	ሚሊፎሊ	Milifoglie cake
Minchet abish wot	የምንቸት አብሽ ወጥ	Spicy ground beef stew
Misa	ምሳ	Lunch
Misir	ምስር	Lentils
Misir alicha wot	የምስር አልጫ ወጥ	Mild lentil stew
Misir shorba	የምስር ሾርባ	Lentil soup
Misir wot	ምስር ወጥ	Lentil stew
Mitmita	ሚጥሚጣ	Spicy blend of peppers
Nech azmud	ነጭ አዝሙድ	Ethiopian white cumin powder/ caraway seed
Nech shinkurt	ነጭ ሽንኩርት	Garlic
Pasta al forno	ፓስታልፎርኖ	One-pot pasta dish
Quanta	ቋንጣ	Beef jerky
Rekebot	ረከቦት	Ethiopian coffee table
Rozmeri	ሮዝሜሪ	Rosemary
Sambusa	ሳምቡሳ	Ethiopian samosa
Senafitch	ሰናፍጭ	Black mustard
Shimbra duket	ሽንብራ ዱቄት	Chickpea flour (ground and unseasoned)
Shiro flour	ሽሮ	Chickpea powder mixed with spices and seasonings
Shiro wot	ሽሮ ወጥ	Chickpea stew
Shorba	ሾርባ	Soup
Siga	ስጋ	Beef
Siga wot	የስጋ ወጥ	Spicy beef stew
Sini	ስኒ	Ethiopian coffee cup
Sinig karia	ስንግ ቃሪያ	Ethiopian stuffed jalapeños
Spris	ስፕሪስ	Ethiopian layered juice

Suf	ሱፍ	Sunflower
Tej	ጠጅ	Ethiopian honey wine
Tella	ጠላ	Ethiopian traditional beer
Telba	ተልባ	Flax seeds
Tenadam	ጤናአዳም	Rue
Tenadam duket	ጤናአዳም ዱቄት	Rue powder
Tibs	ጥብስ	Beef stir-fry
Tikil gomen	ጥቅል ጎመን	Ethiopian cabbage stew
Tikur azmud	ጥቁር አዝሙድ	Black cumin seeds/caraway seeds
Timatim	ቲማቲም	Tomato
Timatim fitfit	ቲማቲም ፍትፍት	Tomato fitfit
Timatim selata	ቲማቲም ሰላጣ	Tomato salad
Timatim with tuna	ቲማቲም ሰላጣ ከቱና ጋር	Tomato salad with tuna
Tiramisu	ቲራሚሱ	Tiramisu
Tosign	ጦስኝ	Thyme
Tosign tea	የጦስኝ ሻይ	Ethiopian thyme tea
Ye asa ena ye dinich shorba	የአሳ እና የድንች ሾርባ	Fish and potato soup
Ye beg alicha wot	የበግ አልጫ ወጥ	Mild lamb stew
Ye beg key wot	የበግ ቀይ ወጥ	Spicy lamb stew
Ye beg kikil	የበግ ቅቅል	Lamb broth stew
Ye beg tibs	የበግ ጥብስ	Lamb stir-fry
Ye beg wot	የበግ ወጥ	Spicy lamb stew
Ye dinich shorba	የድንች ሾርባ	Potato soup
Ye doro wot fitfit	የዶሮ ወጥ ፍትፍት	Chicken fitfit
Ye misir sambusa	የምስር ሳምቡሳ	Lentil samosas
Ye quanta firfir	የቋንጣ ፍርፍር	Ethiopian beef jerky fitfit
Ye siga ena ye atkilit shorba	የሰጋ እና የድንች ሾርባ	Beef and vegetable soup
Ye siga firfir	የሰጋ ፍርፍር	Firfir with beef
Ye suf fitfit	የሱፍ ፍትፍት	Sunflower sauce with injera
Ye telba fitfit	የተልባ ፍትፍት	Flaxseed sauce with injera
Ye tsom migeb	የጾም ምግብ	Lent/fasting food
Zilzil tibs	ዝልዝል ጥብስ	Sliced beef stir-fry
Zinjibil	ዝንጅብል	Ginger

SETTENTRIONALE
HABAB
Mar Ro
BOGOS
Cassala
Adua
Galabat
I. Tana
AMARA
GOGGIAM

መቅያ

Appetizers, Snacks & Side Dishes

Appetizers are not as common in Ethiopian cuisine as they are in Western cuisines, as meals are served family-style on one dish or platter meant for sharing.

However, our side dishes are designed to be enjoyed alone or to spice up any main dish, so all the recipes in this chapter can also be served as appetizers or snacks.

Ye Misir Sambusa (Ethiopian Lentil Samosa)
የምስር ሳምቡሳ

Sambusa is a pastry filled with lentils or beef, similar to the Indian samosa. It was one of my favorite snacks when I was growing up. Actually, it's still a favorite. It is served as an appetizer or snack.

Serves 4–6

1 cup brown lentils

1 medium yellow onion, diced

⅓ cup oil

2 jalapeños, deseeded and diced

2 cloves garlic, diced

1 teaspoon grated ginger

1 teaspoon ground coriander

Salt and pepper

½ (4.7-ounce) package egg roll/spring roll wraps (or 8 sheets of phyllo pastry, halved)

Vegetable oil for frying (about 4 cups)

Place the lentils in a pot, add enough water to cover them by 2 inches, and bring to a boil over medium heat. Cook, stirring occasionally, until the lentils are al dente, about 5 minutes. You don't want them fully cooked or mushy. Remove from the heat, drain, and set aside.

Place the onions and oil in a skillet. Cook over medium heat until the onions are translucent and beginning to brown, about 5 minutes. Stir in the jalapeños, garlic, and ginger. Cook to soften slightly, about 5 minutes. Stir in the lentils and coriander, making sure the coriander does not clump. Turn down the heat to low, add salt and pepper to taste, and stir. Cover the pot and let cook, stirring occasionally, until the lentils are fully cooked, 8–10 minutes. Remove from the heat and set aside.

Working with one egg roll wrapper at time, fold each sheet into a cone and add 2 tablespoons of lentils. Fold in the top edges of the wrapper to close it, brush a little water along each edge, and seal. Repeat the process with the remaining wrappers and filling.

Place 4 cups of oil in a deep, heavy-bottomed pot. The oil should be at least 4 inches deep, but it shouldn't come more than halfway up the sides of the pot, so adjust the amount as required. Place the pot over high heat and bring the oil to boiling point (365°F). Deep-fry a few samubusas at a time, making sure they are submerged in the oil and gently turning them so they cook evenly on each side. Give the oil a few minutes to return to temperature between batches. Once they are golden brown, about 5 minutes, use a slotted spoon to remove them from the pot and place on paper towel or parchment paper to drain the oil.

Serve while warm with a side of sauce—my personal favorites are awaze (page 40) or kochkocha (page 44)—or by itself.

Note: For the meat version of this dish, called ye siga sambusa (beef sambusas) — የስጋ ሳምቡሳ, substitute the lentils with 1 pound of ground beef. Place the beef in a pot and add enough water to cover it by 2 inches. Bring to a boil over medium heat and cook, stirring occasionally, until rare/medium-rare but not fully cooked, about 5 minutes. Remove from the heat, drain, and follow the method above from paragraph 2 to the end.

Timatim Selata (Tomato Salad)
ቲማቲም ሰላጣ

This is a quick and easy salad that pairs well with any main dish. It also makes a great appetizer. While my brother loves the basic tomato salad version, my sister and I love the option of adding lettuce and tuna to turn it into a heartier meal.

Serves 4–6

4 large tomatoes (beefsteak work well), with their seeds, diced

1 medium yellow onion, diced

2 cloves garlic, diced

4 jalapeño peppers (or serrano if you like things extra spicy), deseeded and diced

¼ cup oil

3 tablespoons white vinegar

Salt and pepper

Place the tomatoes, onions, garlic, and jalapeños in a medium bowl and mix well. Add the oil, vinegar, and salt and pepper to taste and mix again. Refrigerate, uncovered, for a minimum of 10 minutes, and no more than 24 hours.

Serve with injera, rice, or your favorite whole grain bread.

Notes:

Add 1 heart of romaine lettuce or half an iceberg lettuce, chopped, before adding the oil and vinegar.

For a heartier version, add 1 can of tuna (white tuna in water works well), drained, when you add the tomatoes.

Homemade Salad Dressing

Makes about 1½ cups

Dressing

½ cup olive oil

½ cup balsamic vinegar

½ cup water

1 tablespoon pepper

2 teaspoons celery seeds

1 tablespoon brown sugar

Salt

This is my mom's recipe for salad dressing. I also use it on salmon and other seafood salad dishes. What can I say? Mom knows best!

Place all the ingredients in a medium bowl and mix well. Pour into an airtight container and refrigerate until needed. This will keep in the fridge for up to 30 days.

Timatim Fitfit (Tomato Fitfit)
ቲማቲም ፍትፍት

Here is another simple everyday salad—with a twist. It's a tomato salad with pieces of injera (page 129). There are various versions of this dish and this one is my mother's recipe. Don't worry, I asked for permission first!

Serves 4–6

2 medium yellow onions, diced

5 cloves garlic, diced

4 jalapeño peppers (or serrano if you like things extra spicy), deseeded and diced

6 large tomatoes (beefsteak work well), with their seeds, diced

1 teaspoons grated ginger

6 tablespoons vegetable oil (or olive oil)

3 tablespoons mayonnaise

1 cup lime juice (about 10 limes) (or 3 tablespoons white vinegar)

Salt

1 large injera

Place the onions, garlic, jalapeños, and tomatoes in a medium bowl and mix well. Add the ginger, oil, and mayonnaise and mix again.

Add the lime juice and salt to taste and mix well. Cover and refrigerate for a minimum of 30 minutes, or up to 2 hours.

Place the injera in a large bowl, tearing it into bite-size pieces. Pour the tomato mixture over the injera. Mix well with your hands or spoon until the sauce is evenly distributed and has soaked into all the pieces of injera.

Serve with more injera, rice, or your favorite whole grain bread.

Ye Asa Ena Ye Dinich Shorba (Fish & Potato Soup)

የአሳ እና የድንች ሾርባ

Looking for a hearty dish that's high in protein and low in fat? This soup is your answer. Another popular dish because of Western influence, the fish and potatoes are a marriage made in heaven. Each mouthful is sure to satisfy your palate and stomach.

Serves 4–6

4 russet potatoes, peeled and cut into 1-inch cubes

1 medium yellow onion, diced

2 tablespoons oil

3 cups water

1 pound firm white fish (halibut, cod, and seabass all work well), cut into 1-inch cubes

2 cups whole milk

¼ cup unsalted butter

1 teaspoon mitmita (optional)

Salt and pepper

Place the potatoes in a pot and add enough water to cover them by 2 inches. Bring to a boil over medium heat. Stir and then cook until they are al dente but not fully cooked or mushy, 5–7 minutes. Remove from the heat, drain, and set aside.

In a separate pot, sauté the onions in the oil over medium heat until they are translucent and beginning to brown, about 5 minutes. Add the water, potatoes, and fish and mix well. Cook, stirring occasionally, until the potatoes are fully cooked, about 10 minutes.

Add the milk, butter, mitmita (if using), and salt and pepper to taste. Mix well, turn down the heat to low, and cook, stirring occasionally, for 5 minutes, just to warm everything through and combine the flavors. Remove from the heat and serve hot.

Misir Shorba (Lentil Soup)
የምስር ሾርባ

Ethiopian cuisine does not really have a tradition of soup, but over the years, due to Western influence, more and more places started serving soup with traditional spices. There is a hotel in Addis that I always love visiting when I go back home that serves an amazing misir shorba. This is my homage to and interpretation of that dish.

Serves 4–6

2 cups brown lentils

1 large yellow onion, diced

3 cloves garlic, diced

3 tablespoons vegetable oil (or olive oil)

2 tablespoons berbere

½ teaspoon ground cumin

1 teaspoon ground ginger

1 (28-ounce) can diced tomatoes

3 cups water

2 dried bay leaves

Salt and pepper

Place the lentils in a pot, add enough water to cover them by 2 inches, and bring to a boil over medium heat. Cook, stirring occasionally, until the lentils are al dente, about 5 minutes. You don't want them fully cooked or mushy. Remove from the heat, drain, and set aside.

Place the onions, garlic, and oil in a pot over medium heat and cook until the vegetables are translucent and beginning to brown, about 5 minutes. Stir in the berbere, cumin, and ginger, making sure the dried spices do not clump up. Stir in the diced tomatoes and their juice, followed by the 3 cups of water. Bring to a boil.

Once the water is boiling, stir in the lentils. Turn down the heat to low, add the bay leaves and salt and pepper to taste, and stir. Cover and let cook, stirring occasionally, until the lentils are fully cooked, 10–15 minutes. Remove from the heat and serve hot.

Ye Siga Ena Ye Atkilit Shorba (Beef & Vegetable Soup)

የስጋ እና የድንች ሾርባ

No one likes being sick, but if there is one thing I looked forward to when I was feeling under the weather, it was my mother making me this soup. Its savory broth, hearty vegetables, and tender beef always seemed to cure anything I had. I enjoy making this dish on weekends because I can warm it up after work for a quick and easy dinner. But even though I now have the recipe, I still ask my mother to make this for me because it always tastes better when it has her special touch.

Serves 4–6

2 russet potatoes, peeled and cut into 1-inch cubes

2 carrots, chopped

1 yellow onion, diced

3 tablespoons oil

½ pound beef (chuck roast or chuck shoulder work well), cubed

1 (14½-ounce) can diced tomatoes

1 jalapeño, deseeded and diced

2 cups water

½ teaspoon ground coriander

1 tablespoon all-purpose flour

1 cup whole milk

Salt and pepper

Place the potatoes and carrots in a large pot and add enough water to cover them by 3 inches. Bring to a boil over medium heat. Stir and cook until they are al dente but not fully cooked or mushy, 5–7 minutes. Remove from the heat, drain, and set aside.

In a separate pot, sauté the onions in the oil over medium heat until they are translucent and beginning to brown, about 5 minutes. Add the beef and cook, stirring occasionally, until the beef is browned on all sides, about 5 minutes. Add the cooked potatoes and carrots, the tomatoes and their juice, and jalapeños and cook, stirring continuously, until the vegetables begin to soften, 5 minutes. Stir in 2 cups of water and the coriander and continue to cook, stirring occasionally, for about 5 minutes, just to warm everything through and combine the flavors.

Stir in the flour and then the milk. Bring to a boil over medium heat and cook for 5 minutes, making sure it stays at a boil. Add salt and pepper to taste, and turn down the heat to low. Cover and cook, stirring occasionally, until the potatoes and carrots are fully cooked and the beef is cooked and tender, about 15 minutes. Serve hot.

Dabo Kolo

ዳቦ ቆሎ

This snack is traditionally served at our Ethiopian coffee ceremony (page 147) or with tea. It's also a go-to snack to serve when guests come over. I was notorious for grabbing this when my mom wasn't looking.

Serves 4–6

2 cups all-purpose flour

1 tablespoon sugar

1 tablespoon berbere

1 teaspoon salt

½ cup warm water (hand-hot)

1 cup oil

Mix together the flour, sugar, berbere, and salt in a medium bowl. Pour in the water, and mix well to combine. Once the dough is smooth, lump-free, and similar to bread dough, break off tennis ball–sized pieces and roll them out into long cylinders, no more than 1 inch in diameter. (If the dough is too dry, add about 1 tablespoon of water. If it is too wet, add about 1 tablespoon of flour.) Cut the rolls into ½-inch pieces.

Place the oil in a deep pot and bring it to 375°F over medium-high heat. Working in batches, fry the dough until golden brown on all sides, 3–4 minutes in total. Remove from the heat and place on paper towel to drain off any excess oil. Let the oil come back to temperature and then repeat with the remaining dough.

Once cool to the touch, enjoy with an Ethiopian coffee or alone as a snack.

Note: For a fun-colored snack, add a pinch of turmeric or food coloring to the flour to change the color of the dabo kolo.

Chiko

ጭኮ

Chiko, or Ethiopian chocolate as I used to call it as a child, is a thick and creamy snack. Traditionally served with coffee, this dish is consumed both as an everyday treat and on holidays and for ceremonies.

Serves 4–6

2 cups beso duket

1 teaspoon caraway seeds

1 teaspoon ground coriander

1 teaspoon ground cardamom

1 teaspoon salt

1 cup melted kibe

Place the beso duket, caraway seed, coriander, cardamom, and salt in a bowl and mix together. Slowly add the melted kibe and mix until smooth and lump-free.

Transfer the dough to a flat pan or container (a rectangular 32 ounce/8.75- × 6-inch plastic container works well), making sure to press it down right into the corners. Seal and cover with plastic wrap and refrigerate for a minimum of 1 hour or until it hardens. Cut it into 1- to 2-inch squares, triangles, or small shapes of your choice and enjoy with an Ethiopian coffee or tea.

Awaze (Ethiopian Hot Sauce)

አዋዜ

Awaze is used to accompany and spice up any dish. Known as Ethiopian hot sauce, it may also be eaten alongside injera (page 129) as a snack. I put it on everything, but my personal favorites to pair this dish with are tibs (beef stir-fry, page 113) and tire siga (a raw meat dish). Every household has its own recipe for awaze. Here I've given you my mom's recipe followed by mine. Both will keep for up to 30 days stored in an airtight container in the fridge.

Awaze #1

Makes about 1 cup

5 cloves garlic, diced

1 teaspoon grated ginger

1 tablespoon ground cardamom

1 cup water

1 cup berbere

2 tablespoons lime juice (about 1 lime)

1 tablespoon oil

2 teaspoons salt

Place the garlic, ginger, cardamom, and water in a small pot, bring to a boil over medium heat, and keep at a boil for 10 minutes, stirring occasionally. Remove from the heat and let sit for 5 minutes. Once the ingredients have settled on the bottom of the pot, strain the water through a fine mesh sieve into a medium bowl and discard the solids.

Stir the berbere into the water, mixing well so the berbere does not clump up. Add warm water as needed, about 1 tablespoon at a time, if the mixture is too thick. Once the mixture is smooth, add the lime juice, oil, and then the salt. Mix again, taste, and add more salt if needed. Refrigerate in an airtight container for a minimum of 20 minutes before using.

Serve on the side with your favorite Ethiopian wot or to spice up any dish.

Awaze #2

Makes about 2 cups

1 cup berbere

½ teaspoon ground cardamom

¼ cup red wine (recommend a cabernet or merlot) or whisky (recommend Johnnie Walker)

1 cup warm water (hand-hot)

Salt and pepper

Mix the ingredients in a medium bowl until smooth.
Serve on the side with your favorite Ethiopian wot or to spice up any dish.

Note: Johnnie Walker is the whisky of choice among Ethiopians. Whether it is an event like a wedding or a birthday party, or company is coming over, Johnnie Walker is guaranteed to be one of the options on offer alongside wine, tej (page 153), and soft drinks. I'm not sure why, but for as long as I can remember, it has been the preferred whisky among the Abesha community. My personal favorite is Johnnie Walker Blue Label, which I especially enjoy with my friends every year on my birthday.

Ayib (Ethiopian Cheese)
አይብ

Ayib is often referred to as Ethiopian feta cheese. Most commonly served with doro wot (page 95) or kitfo (page 99), it is served as a side to cool down our spiciest dishes. This will keep in an airtight container in the fridge for up to 2 weeks.

Makes about 6–8 servings

1 gallon (19 cups) buttermilk

2 cups white vinegar

Place the milk in a medium pot and bring to a boil over low heat. Once it reaches a boil, slowly add the vinegar, stirring continuously until the mixture becomes frothy. Remove from the heat and set aside to cool in the pot to room temperature. Transfer to an airtight container and store in a dry spot at room temperature for a minimum of 12 hours, and up to 24 hours. (Do not refrigerate, as it won't ferment quickly enough.)

After the 12 hours, drain off the water on top of the cheese. Wrap the cheese in a piece of cheesecloth and squeeze out all the water. Place the cheese in a bowl, cover, and refrigerate for 12 hours before using. (If you're short of time, you can refrigerate for only 2 hours but I really don't recommend that option.)

Serve on the side with your favorite Ethiopian dish or salad.

Sinig Karia (Ethiopian Stuffed Jalapeño)
ስንግ ቃሪያ

I love spicy food, as anyone who knows me will attest. And although most of our dishes are already spice-forward, this dish helps add another kick to any meal. I can eat sinig karia with anything, including non-Ethiopian dishes. My mother always makes the best kind, and every time she makes it, you can guarantee my siblings and I will be fighting over it.

Serves 4–6

1 medium yellow (or red) onion, diced

3 cloves garlic, diced

2 large tomatoes (beefsteak work well), seeds discarded, diced

¼ cup vegetable oil (or olive oil)

2 tablespoons white vinegar

Salt

6 large jalapeño peppers

Place the onions, garlic, and tomatoes in a medium bowl and mix well. Add the oil, vinegar, and salt to taste and mix again.

Next, cut the jalapeños vertically but without cutting all the way through. You want them to open like a book. Keep the stem intact, so you can use it hold the pepper. Discard all the seeds. Stuff the jalapeños with the vegetable mixture.

Serve with your favorite Ethiopian wot or on the side to spice up any dish.

Kochkocha (Ethiopian Jalapeño Hot Sauce)

ቆጭቆጫ

A milder hot sauce, kochkocha is most commonly served with dabo (bread), tibs (beef stir-fry, page 113), and sambusa (page 29). Also known as ye karia deleh or ye karia awaze, kochkocha is viewed as the salsa verde of Ethiopia. This can be stored in an airtight container in the fridge for up to 2 weeks.

Makes about 6–8 servings

- 15 large jalapeño peppers
- 5 serrano peppers (or habanero if you like things spicy)
- 2 medium white onions, diced
- 1 tablespoon grated ginger
- 1 bunch flat-leaf parsley (or cilantro)
- 1 teaspoon dried oregano leaves
- ½ teaspoon ground cardamom
- ½ teaspoon ground cumin
- ¼ cup olive oil
- ¼ cup lime juice (about 3 limes)
- Salt and pepper

Cut the jalapeños and serranos in half and discard all their seeds and ribs. Halve them again and place them in a blender or food processor fitted with a steel blade. Add the onions, ginger, parsley, oregano, cardamom, cumin, oil, lime juice, and salt and pepper to taste, and blend until smooth (some lumps are okay).

Serve with sambusa or on the side to spice up any dish.

Ergo (Ethiopian Yogurt)
እርጎ

A traditional homemade Ethiopian fermented milk, ergo is like a yogurty sour cream. We use this dish to cool down our spiciest meals like doro wot (page 95) and siga wot (page 107). This dish is most commonly served at events, on holidays, and at celebrations. This will keep in an airtight container in the fridge for up to 2 weeks.

Makes about 6–8 servings

10 cups whole milk

3 tablespoons sour cream

1 sprig rue plant (optional)

Place the milk in a medium pot and bring to a boil over low heat, stirring continuously. Once the milk comes to a boil, remove from the heat and let cool in the pot for 15 minutes.

Transfer to an airtight container, add the sour cream, and mix well. Place the rue plant on top for garnish and flavoring (if using). Cover and set aside in a dry spot at room temperature for 24 hours. (Do not refrigerate, as it won't ferment quickly enough.)

Serve on the side of your favorite Ethiopian dish or salad.

Note: Rue plant, also known as herb-of-grace, is an herb that is commonly used in Ethiopian yogurt and coffee. It has strong aromatic qualities and a little goes a very long way. It was very popular in the past for traditional medicinal purposes and as an ornamental plant for herb gardening. When I was growing up, we had this fragrant plant in our garden, which was very convenient if we wanted to use it during coffee ceremonies or for making ergo. Nowadays, I tend to find the plant at garden centers, farmers' markets, or online.

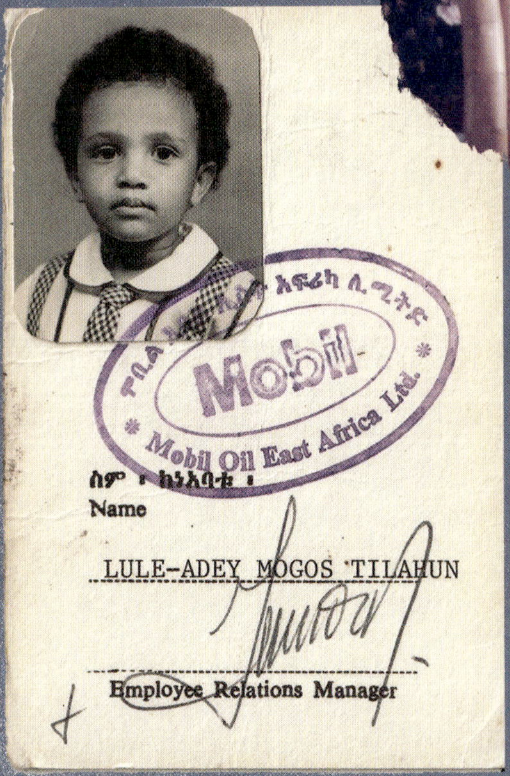
Mobil
Mobil Oil East Africa Ltd.
ስም ፡ ከነአባቱ ፡
Name
LULE-ADEY MOGOS TILAHUN
Employee Relations Manager

ቁርስ

Breakfast Dishes

Ethiopian cuisine does not typically have dishes that are specifically for breakfast. While we have some common breakfast items like scrambled eggs, breakfast is usually any main dish served with injera.

Firfir (Ethiopian Breakfast Scramble)

ፍርፍር

***Firfir* means to mix or scramble. A light and simple dish with minimal ingredients, it is my go-to quick meal recipe. I enjoy this dish especially when it's paired with quanta (Ethiopian beef jerky).**

Serves 2

1 large yellow onion, diced

4 tablespoons vegetable oil (or 2 tablespoons kibe)

1 teaspoon grated ginger

3 cloves garlic, diced

3 tablespoons berbere

1 cup water

3 jalapeños, deseeded and thinly sliced

Salt and pepper

1 large injera (page 129, or ½ pound dirkosh, dry injera)

Place the onions in a medium pot, add the oil, and cook over medium heat until they are translucent and beginning to brown, about 5 minutes. Stir in the ginger and garlic and cook until just beginning to soften, 4 minutes.

Add the berbere and water and bring to a boil, stirring constantly. Add the jalapeños and salt and pepper to taste and mix well. Turn down the heat to low and cook until the sauce has thickened enough to coat the back of a spoon, about 5 minutes. Remove from the heat.

Tear the injera into bite-size pieces and add them to the pot. Mix well until the sauce is evenly distributed and has soaked into all the pieces of injera, about 2 minutes.

Serve hot with more injera or your favorite whole grain bread.

Notes:

For my favorite version, tear ½ pound of quanta into bite-size pieces and add it when you add the injera.

Dirkosh is a dried form of injera. Traditionally, we make dirkosh by laying injera on a tarp outside and letting the sun do all of the work. Another option is to bake the injera on low heat (around 275°F) in the oven for about an hour or in a dehydrator (check the instructions of your dehydrator for guidance). You can brush the injera lightly with oil first if you like.

Ye Siga Firfir (Firfir with Beef)
የስጋ ፍርፍር

Ye siga firfir is a great way to use leftover injera (page 129). Most commonly served for brunch and breakfast, it makes a great pairing with enqulal fifir (Ethiopian scrambled eggs, page 53) and kinche (page 57), served on a platter to eat together as a family.

Serves 4–6

2 medium yellow onions, diced

4 tablespoons vegetable oil (or 2 tablespoons kibe)

1 pound beef, cubed (bottom round or top round work well)

2 teaspoons grated ginger

4 cloves garlic, diced

3 tablespoons berbere

2 cups water

Salt and pepper

2 large injera (or ½ pound dirkosh, dry injera)

Place the onions in a medium pot, add the oil, and cook over medium heat until the onions are translucent and beginning to brown, about 5 minutes. Stir in the beef and cook, stirring occasionally, until the meat is browned on all sides, about 5 minutes. Stir in the ginger and garlic and cook until just beginning to soften, about 4 minutes.

Add the berbere and water and stir, still over medium heat, until it comes to a boil. Add salt and pepper to taste and mix well. Turn down the heat to low and cook until the sauce has thickened enough to coat the back of a spoon, about 10 minutes. Remove from the heat.

Tear the injera into bite-size pieces and add it to the pot. Mix well until the sauce is evenly distributed and has soaked into all the pieces of injera, about 2 minutes.

Serve with more injera or your favorite whole grain bread.

Enqulal Firfir (Ethiopian Scrambled Eggs)
እንቁላል ፍርፍር

Many cultures have a version of scrambled eggs, but none satisfies my palate like the Ethiopian version. I have fond memories of my childhood back in Addis, starting my day with this dish in the mornings before school, or enjoying it between bread, as a sandwich, for my afternoon snacks (which we call *mekses*).

Serves 4–6

6 tablespoons vegetable oil (or olive oil)

1 medium yellow (or red) onion, roughly chopped

3 cloves garlic, diced

1 large tomato (beefsteak tomato works well), with seeds, diced

1 teaspoon grated ginger

6 eggs

Salt and pepper

2 jalapeño peppers (or serrano if you like things extra spicy), deseeded and diced

In a medium pan or skillet, warm the oil over medium heat. Add the onions and garlic and cook until the onions are translucent and beginning to brown, about 5 minutes.

Add the tomatoes and ginger and mix well. Cover and cook, stirring occasionally, until the tomatoes are fully cooked, 4 minutes.

Meanwhile, in a medium bowl, lightly whisk the eggs together. Add salt and pepper to taste and whisk to combine.

Add the eggs to the pan and stir. Cover, stirring occasionally, to partly cook the eggs, about 5 minutes. Add the jalapeños and additional salt and pepper to taste (if needed). Mix well and cook the eggs to your liking, about 4 minutes or longer.

Serve hot with injera or your favorite whole grain bread.

Note: Add this to lightly toasted bread and make breakfast sandwiches.

Chechebsa (Ethiopian Breakfast Dish)

ጨጨብሳ

I think of this as the perfect brunch meal: spicy, filling, and fun to eat. Chechebsa is a simple dish with bold flavors and spices that is traditionally served with coffee or tea. Think of it as a spicy and savory Ethiopian bread pudding!

Serves 4–6

- 3 cups bread flour
- 3 cups water
- 1 teaspoon salt
- 1 cup olive oil (or ½ cup kibe, melted)
- 1 tablespoon berbere

In a medium bowl, whisk the flour with the water until you get a smooth batter (the consistency of pancake batter). Add the salt, mix well, and set aside.

In a large skillet, warm 1 teaspoon of the oil over medium heat. Slowly add about ½ cup of batter to thinly coat the bottom of the skillet. Cook until the underside is light brown, 2–4 minutes, and flip to opposite side and cook until the batter is cooked through, 2–4 minutes. Remove from the heat and place on paper towel to absorb any excess oil. Repeat with the remaining batter, using 1 teaspoon of oil each time. These are your kita.

In a separate bowl, mix the remaining oil with the berbere until smooth.

Tear all the kita into 1-inch pieces and place them in a large bowl. Pour the oil and berbere mixture over top and mix to coat all the pieces. Fluff with a fork. Serve warm.

Note: Chechebsa is also known as kita firfir. *Firfir* means to scramble or mix, and when the thin bread is cooked, it turns into kita bread. When you cut it into pieces and mix it, it is kita firfir.

Kinche (Ethiopian Cracked Wheat)
ቅንጬ

One of my brother's favorite dishes is kinche. It is traditionally served for breakfast, but he enjoys it anytime of day. You will almost always find this dish served for breakfast at my mother's house, paired with firfir (page 51) and enqulal firfir (page 53), which complement each other so well.

Serves 4–6

2 cups kinche

4 cups water

Salt

2 tablespoons olive oil (or 1 tablespoon kibe, melted)

Rinse the kinche in a stainless steel fine mesh strainer until the water runs clear and set aside.

In a medium pot, bring the water to a boil over high heat. Add the rinsed kinche and salt to taste. Turn down the heat to medium, cover, and cook until the kinche is fluffy and tender, 10–15 minutes.

Remove from the heat, mix in the oil, and fluff with a fork. Let sit for 5 minutes before serving.

Genfo (Ethiopian Porridge)

ገንፎ

This dish reminds me of Ethiopian winters, also known as the rainy season. There is nothing better than eating a bowl of genfo and then lying down for a rest while listening to the sound of rain. Oh, how I miss and long for those days . . .

Serves 4–6

4 cups water

1 teaspoon salt

3 cups barley flour

3 tablespoons melted kibe (or 3 tablespoons olive oil)

1 tablespoon berbere

In a medium pot, mix together the water and salt and then bring to a boil over medium heat. Once the water is boiling, slowly add the flour, stirring constantly with a wooden spoon. Mix well to remove any lumps. The mixture will be thick, so add water, about 1 tablespoon at a time, if needed. Remove from the heat and set aside. This is the genfo.

Place the genfo in a small bowl and create a well in the center. Pour in the melted butter and then the berbere. Mix well. Serve immediately while it is still hot.

Bula Genfo (Bula Porridge Dish)
የቡላ ገንፎ

Looking for a hearty breakfast? Well, look no further. Bula is rich in calcium, iron, and carbohydrates. This rib-sticking breakfast dish is guaranteed to keep you warm in the winter or other cold months.

Serves 4–6

1 cup bula powder

2 cups milk

1 teaspoon sugar

1 teaspoon salt

2 tablespoons kibe, melted, divided

1 teaspoon berbere

Whisk together the bula powder, milk, sugar, and salt in a medium bowl.

Once you have a lump-free batter, transfer it to a medium pot and cook on medium heat, stirring constantly, until thick, about 5 minutes. It should not be pourable. Next add 1 tablespoon of the kibe and mix again to combine.

Place the bula in a small bowl and make a well in the center. Add the rest of the kibe to the well, followed by the berbere, and mix well. Serve immediately while it is still hot.

Note: Bula is made from enset root, which is an important food source in Ethiopia. The enset plant is also known as false banana. The powder makes stiff porridge-like dish like bula genfo or can be consumed as a hot beverage like atmit (page 151).

Ful (Spicy Ethiopian Fava Beans)

ፉል

Here is another perfect breakfast or brunch dish for everyone to enjoy. Rich in flavor and umami, ful is a popular dish in both Africa and the Middle East. And if you're like me and enjoy breakfast dishes anytime of the day, feel free to have this for lunch or dinner.

Serves 4–6

- 1 (14-ounce) can fava beans, drained and rinsed
- 1 medium yellow (or red) onion, diced
- 3 tablespoon vegetable oil (or olive oil)
- 1 teaspoon grated ginger
- 4 cloves garlic, diced
- 1 medium tomato (Roma work well), with its seeds, chopped
- 2 teaspoons berbere
- ½ teaspoon ground cumin
- 2 jalapeños, deseeded and diced
- Salt
- 2 tablespoons (total) chopped onions, tomatoes, and jalapeños, for garnish (optional)

Place the fava beans in a small pot and add enough water to cover them by 2 inches. Bring to a boil over medium heat. Stir and then cook until the beans are fully cooked and mushy, about 8–10 minutes. Remove from the heat, drain, mash the beans, and set aside.

In a medium skillet, add the onions and oil and cook over medium heat until the onions are translucent and beginning to brown, about 5 minutes. Add the ginger and garlic and cook, stirring, until just beginning to soften, about 4 minutes

Add the tomatoes, berbere, and cumin, stirring well so the dried spices do not clump up. Cook until the spices are cooked and the tomatoes begin to soften, about 4 minutes. Add the jalapeños and cook until softened, about 3 minutes.

Add the fava beans and salt to taste and mix well by mashing the beans and incorporating them into the sauce. Cook for 3 minutes, stirring continuously, just to warm everything through and combine the flavors. Remove from the heat and garnish with the onions, tomatoes, and jalapeños (if using).

Serve with French bread or your favorite whole grain bread.

Note: You can also top this with a hard-boiled egg cut in half.

የጾም ምግብ

Vegetarian & Vegan Dishes

Ethiopian dishes very commonly include meat but some vegetarian and vegan dishes are traditionally served during Lent and other fasting times. These dishes are also served and enjoyed throughout the year for any meal or occasion.

Misir Wot (Lentil Stew)
ምስር ወጥ

Here is another simple everyday dish that everyone can put their own spin on. I learned this version from my auntie, whom I often stayed with as a child. She makes the best misir wot ever. (Shhh—don't tell my mom I said that!)

Serves 4–6

1 cup red lentils

1 medium yellow onion, diced

3 cloves garlic, diced

⅔ cup vegetable oil (or olive oil)

3 tablespoons berbere

1 cup water

Salt

Place the lentils in a medium pot and add enough water to cover them by 2 inches. Bring to a boil over medium heat. Stir and then cook until the lentils are al dente, about 5 minutes. You don't want them fully cooked or mushy. Remove from the heat, drain, and set aside.

In a separate medium pot, place the onions, garlic, and oil and cook over medium heat until the onions and garlic are translucent and beginning to brown, about 5 minutes. Next, stir in the berbere, making sure it does not clump up. Add 1 cup of water and bring to a boil.

When the water reaches a boil, stir in the lentils. Turn down the heat to low, add salt to taste, and stir. Cover the wot (stew) and cook, stirring occasionally, until the lentils are fully cooked, 15–20 minutes.

Serve hot with injera, rice, or your favorite whole grain bread.

Note: The milder version of this dish is called misir alicha wot (mild lentil stew) — የምስር አልጫ ወጥ. Simply use 1 teaspoon of ground turmeric instead of the berbere and follow the recipe as above.

Shiro Wot (Chickpea Stew)
ሽሮ ወጥ

If there's a dish that made me fall in love with food, this is it. In Ethiopia, it's a staple. Everyone makes it, but no one makes it the way my grandmother did when I was a kid. She had a magical touch that lifted her version above everyone else's . . . When I think of her shiro wot, the years fall away, my mouth starts watering, and I'm back in Addis Ababa, watching her lovingly stir her pot.

Serves 4–6

1 cup shiro flour

4 cups water, divided

1 medium yellow onion, diced

3 tablespoons oil

2 teaspoons grated ginger

3 cloves garlic, diced

1 tablespoon berbere

Salt and pepper

Place the shiro flour in a medium bowl, add 3 cups of the water, and mix well. Stir until it is lump-free and then set aside.

Place the onions and oil in a medium pot and cook over medium heat until they are translucent and beginning to brown, about 5 minutes. Stir in the ginger and garlic and cook until just beginning to soften, about 4 minutes. Stir in the berbere, making sure the powder does not clump. Add the remaining 1 cup of water and bring to a boil.

Add the shiro mixture to the boiling water and stir. Turn down the heat to low, add salt and pepper to taste, and stir. Cover the pot and let the wot cook, stirring occasionally and adding about 1 tablespoon of water at a time, but no more than ½ cup (if required), until the liquid is reduced by about half and the sauce is moderately thick, 20–25 minutes.

Serve hot with injera or your favorite whole grain bread.

Tikil Gomen (Ethiopian Cabbage Stew)
ጥቅል ጎመን

I enjoy tikil gomen, one of my favorite light and healthy dishes, with injera (page 129) or over rice. It also pairs really well with a spicy wot (page 107). This is a popular dish to serve during Lent and other fasting times.

Serves 4–6

- 1 medium yellow onion, diced
- ½ cup vegetable oil
- 2 cloves garlic, diced
- 3 Yukon gold potatoes, peeled and chopped into 1-inch cubes
- 3 carrots, chopped into 1- to 2-inch pieces
- 2 teaspoons ground turmeric
- Salt and pepper
- ½ cup water
- 1 head green cabbage, roughly chopped into bite-size pieces
- 2 medium jalapeño peppers, deseeded and thinly sliced

In a medium pot over medium heat, sauté the onions with the oil. When they start to turn golden brown, about 10 minutes, add the garlic and chopped potatoes and cook, stirring occasionally, until the garlic has started to cook and the potatoes have started to cook on each side, about 5 minutes in total.

Next, add the carrots, turmeric, and salt and pepper to taste and stir for 1 minute. Add the water and bring to a boil, stirring occasionally.

Add the cabbage and jalapeños and mix well. Cover the pan, turn down the heat to low, and simmer, stirring occasionally, until the vegetables are soft, 10–15 minutes.

Serve hot with injera, rice, or whole grain bread.

Note: Napa and Savoy cabbage both work in this recipe, but Savoy is best.

Fossolia (Ethiopian-Style Green Beans)
ፎሶሊያ

This is a popular dish to serve as a side at events and parties. I also enjoy making it when I'm looking for a light, healthy main dish.

Serves 4–6

2 pounds green beans

5 tablespoons vegetable oil (or olive oil)

2 pounds carrots, thinly sliced into rounds

1 medium yellow onion, thinly sliced

4 cloves garlic, finely chopped

1 teaspoon grated ginger

3 medium jalapeño, deseeded and thinly sliced

1 teaspoon ground coriander

½ cup water

Salt and pepper

Place the green beans in a medium pot and add enough water to cover them by 1 inch. Bring to a boil over medium heat. As soon as the water starts to boil, turn down the heat to a simmer and stir. Cook the green beans until they are al dente, about 5 minutes. You don't want them fully cooked or mushy. Remove from the heat, drain, and set aside.

Place the oil and carrots in a skillet and cook over medium heat, stirring, just until they start to soften, about 5 minutes. Stir in the onions, garlic, and ginger. Cook, stirring constantly, until the onions begin to soften and turn translucent, 5–10 minutes. Add the green beans, jalapeños, and coriander and mix well.

Add the ½ cup of water and salt and pepper to taste. Cover the skillet, turn down the heat to low, and let simmer, stirring occasionally, until most of the water has evaporated and the vegetables are cooked through, about 5 minutes.

Serve hot with injera, rice, or your favorite whole grain bread.

Azifa (Lentil Salad)

አዚፋ

Traditionally served during Lent and other fasting times, this dish is quick and easy to prepare. It's also a great dish to prep on a weekend and enjoy throughout the week, as it only tastes better the longer it marinates.

Serves 4–6

2 cups brown lentils

1 medium yellow (or red) onion, diced

4 cloves garlic, diced

4 jalapeños, deseeded and diced

1 teaspoon grated ginger

¾ cup lime juice (about 6 limes)

3 tablespoons vegetable oil (or olive oil)

Salt

Place the lentils in a medium pot and add enough water to cover them by 2 inches. Bring to a boil over medium heat. Stir and then cook until the lentils are fully cooked, 25–30 minutes. Remove from the heat, drain, and set aside.

Place the onions, garlic, and jalapeños in a medium bowl and mix well. Add the ginger, lime juice, oil, and salt to taste and mix again.

Next, add the lentils (they'll be around room-temperature at this point) to the bowl. Mix well and refrigerate, either covered or uncovered, for a minimum of 30 minutes, or up to overnight.

Serve with injera, rice, or your favorite whole grain bread.

Duba Wot (Pumpkin Stew)

የዱባ ወጥ

Popular during Lent and other fasting periods, this spice-forward dish is light and healthy, despite being a stew. I started making this as a meat substitute for my vegetarian friends, and now it's frequently requested by my entire friend group.

Serves 4–6

2 medium yellow onions, diced

3 cloves garlic, diced

¼ cup vegetable oil (or olive oil)

2 tablespoons berbere

1 teaspoons grated ginger

3 large tomatoes (beefsteak work well), with their seeds, diced

2 pounds pumpkin or butternut squash, peeled, deseeded, and cut into 1-inch cubes

1 cup water

½ cup white cooking wine (optional)

3 jalapeño peppers (or serrano if you like things extra spicy), deseeded and diced

Salt

Place the onions, garlic, and oil in a medium pot. Cook over medium heat until the onions are translucent and beginning to brown, about 5 minutes. Stir in the berbere and ginger, making sure the berbere does not clump up. Stir and then cook for 2 minutes. Mix in the tomatoes and cook to soften them a little, about 5 minutes.

Stir in the pumpkin, 1 cup of water, and cooking wine (if using). Cover and let cook, stirring occasionally, until the sauce thickens, 15–20 minutes. Add the jalapeños and salt to taste, stir, and let cook for an additional 5 minutes, just to warm everything through and let the flavors combine.

Serve hot with injera, rice, or your favorite whole grain bread.

Buticha (Ethiopian Chickpea Dish)

ቡጥቻ

A friend introduced me to this dish a couple of years ago and now I can't stop making it. It's easy to make, filling, and healthy, making it a perfect dish after a long day of work.

Serves 4–6

2 cups shimbra duket

Salt

2 cups warm water (hand-hot)

1 medium yellow onion, diced

¼ cup vegetable oil (or olive oil)

4 cloves garlic, diced

½ teaspoon ground turmeric

1 tomato, diced (Roma work well), seeds discarded (optional)

1 jalapeño, deseeded and diced

In a medium bowl, whisk together the shimbra duket, salt to taste, and the water until the mixture is smooth and lump-free.

Place a medium pot over medium heat and add the shimbra duket mixture. Cook, stirring constantly, until fully cooked, 10–15 minutes. The mixture will be thick, so add water, about 1 tablespoon at a time, as needed while it cooks. It should have the consistency of very thick mashed potatoes. Remove from the heat and set aside to cool.

In a medium pan, add the onions and oil and cook over medium heat until they are translucent and beginning to brown, about 5 minutes. Next, add the garlic and turmeric, stir, and let cook for 2 minutes. Add the tomato, jalapeños, and salt to taste and cook, stirring occasionally, for 3 minutes, just to warm everything through and combine the flavors.

Using a fork or your hands, crush the shimbra duket mixture and add to the pan. Cook, stirring occasionally, for another 5 minutes, just to warm through, combine all the flavors, and let the shimbra duket mixture soak up all the oil.

Serve with injera, rice, or your favorite whole grain bread.

Gomen Wot (Collard Greens Stew)

ጎመን ወጥ

This wholesome stew is my go-to when I'm craving some greens in my diet. It's not too spicy and it's meat free. It's also a versatile dish that you can have over rice as a simple lunch or use to accompany something hot and spicy if you're entertaining.

Serves 4–6

1 pound collard greens, rinsed and roughly chopped

1 medium yellow onion, diced

½ cup oil

2 teaspoons grated ginger

3 cloves garlic, diced

1 cup water

3 jalapeños, deseeded and thinly sliced (or 1 green bell pepper, diced)

Salt

Place the collard greens in a medium pot and add enough water to cover them by 3 inches. Bring to a boil over medium heat. Cover and cook, keeping them at a boil, until tender, 15–20 minutes. Remove from the heat, drain, and set aside.

Meanwhile, place the onions and oil in a separate medium pot. Cook over medium heat until they are translucent and beginning to brown, about 5 minutes. Add the ginger and garlic, stir, and cook for 2 minutes. Next, add the greens and 1 cup of water and cook, stirring occasionally, on medium heat until the water has evaporated and the greens are cooked, 10–12 minutes.

Stir in the jalapeños. Turn down the heat to low, add salt to taste, and stir. Cover and let cook, stirring occasionally, until the liquid is reduced and the peppers are soft, 5–10 minutes.

Serve with injera, rice, or your favorite whole grain bread.

Note: The meat version of this is called gomen besega (collard greens with beef stew) — ጎመን በስጋ. Place 2 pounds of chuck roast beef (or your favorite lean beef), cut in 1- to 2-inch cubes, in a medium pot and add enough water to cover the ingredients by 2 inches. Bring to a boil over medium heat and cook, stirring occasionally, until the beef is rare to medium-rare but not fully cooked. Remove from the heat, drain, and set aside. Follow the same recipe above, adding the meat when you add the collard greens in paragraph 2.

Key Sir (Ethiopian Beets and Potatoes)
ቀይ ስር

Popular among vegetarians and vegans, key sir can be served warm or cold. It is also another dish commonly eaten during fasting periods. One of my favorite childhood memories is of peeling the beets for this dish for my aunts and scaring my parents when they saw my red hands.

Serves 4–6

4 large beets, peeled and chopped in 1-inch cubes

3 large Yukon gold potatoes

1 pound carrots, chopped into 1- to 2-inch pieces

3 tablespoons vegetable oil (or olive oil)

1 medium yellow onion, diced

3 cloves garlic, diced

1 teaspoon grated ginger

Salt and pepper

Place the beets in a medium pot and add enough water to cover them by 2 inches. Bring to a boil over medium heat and keep them at a boil until al dente, about 5 minutes. You don't want them fully cooked or mushy. Remove from the heat, drain, and set aside.

Place the potatoes in a small pot and add enough water to cover them by 2 inches. Bring to a boil over medium heat and keep them at a boil until fork-tender, about 10 minutes. Drain and let cool enough to touch, then peel and chop them into 1-inch cubes and set aside.

Place the carrots in a separate small pot and add enough water to cover them by 1 inch. Bring to a boil over medium heat and keep them at a boil until just soft, about 8 minutes. Remove from the heat, drain, and set aside.

In a large skillet or pot, add the oil and beets and place over medium-high heat. Cook, stirring occasionally, on all sides until the beets have softened, about 4 minutes. Mix in the onions, garlic, and ginger and cook, stirring occasionally, until the onions are translucent and beginning to brown, about 5 minutes. Add the potatoes, carrots, and salt and pepper to taste, mix well, and cook for 5 minutes, just to warm everything through and let the flavors combine.

Serve hot with injera, rice, or your favorite whole grain bread.

Ater Kik Alicha Wot
(Mild Yellow Split Pea Stew)
የአተር ክክ አልጫ ወጥ

A very tasty and nutritious dish, ater kik is one of our mildest wots and is safe to serve to people who don't enjoy spicy foods. Traditionally we serve this dish to children until they're ready to graduate to the spicier stuff. My niece and nephew love it when my mom makes this for them because no one makes anything like Grandma does!

Serves 4–6

1 cup dried yellow split peas

1 medium yellow onion, diced

3 cloves garlic, diced

⅔ cup vegetable oil (or olive oil)

1 teaspoon ground turmeric

1 cup water

Salt

Place the split peas in a medium pot and add enough water to cover them by 2 inches. Bring to a boil over medium heat. Stir and keep at a boil until the split peas are al dente. You don't want them fully cooked or mushy. Remove from the heat, drain, and set aside.

Meanwhile, in a separate medium pot, add the onions, garlic, and oil and cook over medium heat until the onions and garlic are translucent and beginning to brown, about 5 minutes. Stir in the turmeric, making sure the powder does not clump. Add 1 cup of water and bring to a boil, still over medium heat.

Add the split peas to the boiling sauce and stir. Turn down the heat to low, add salt to taste, and stir. Cover and let cook, stirring occasionally, until the split peas are fully cooked, 15–20 minutes.

Serve hot with injera, rice, or your favorite whole grain bread.

Ye Suf Fitfit (Sunflower Sauce with Injera)
የሱፍ ፍትፍት

A very satisfying meal, suf fitfit is the perfect dish for Lent or other fasting periods. It is also a great vegan meal.

Serves 4–6

1 cup sunflower seeds

2 cups water, divided

3 medium yellow onions, diced

2 jalapeño peppers, deseeded and diced

3 pieces rue leaf (see note on page 45), chopped

Salt

1 large injera (page 129)

Rinse the sunflower seeds, place them in a medium pot, and add enough water to cover them by 2 inches. Bring to a boil over medium heat. Stir and keep at a boil until the seeds are soft, 10–15 minutes. Remove from the heat, drain, and set aside.

Transfer to a blender or food processor fitted with a steel blade. Add 1 cup of the water and blend until all the seeds are fully processed. Strain through a fine mesh sieve into a bowl, pressing down so you get all the liquid out, and discard any sediment.

Add the onions, jalapeños, rue, and the remaining 1 cup of water to the bowl of sunflower liquid and mix well. Add salt to taste and mix well again. Cover and refrigerate for a minimum of 10 minutes, or up to overnight.

Tear the injera into bite-size pieces and place them in a large bowl. Pour the sunflower mixture over the injera. Mix well until the sauce is evenly distributed and has soaked into all the pieces of injera.

Serve with more injera or your favorite whole grain bread.

Ye Telba Fitfit (Flaxseed Sauce with Injera)
የተልባ ፍትፍት

Have a vegan friend who doesn't like spicy food? This creamy dish is guaranteed to satisfy their palate and as a bonus, it is healthy and a great source of vitamin B.

Serves 4–6

1 cup ground flaxseed

1 ½ cups water

2 tablespoons olive oil

1 medium yellow onion, diced

3 jalapeño peppers, deseeded and diced

Salt

1 large injera (page 129)

In a medium bowl, mix the ground flaxseed and water. Add the oil, onions, jalapeños, and salt to taste and mix again.

Tear the injera into bite-size pieces and place them in a large bowl. Pour the flaxseed mixture over the injera. Mix well until the sauce is evenly distributed and has soaked into all the pieces of injera.

Serve with more injera or your favorite whole grain bread.

Vegetarian Lasagna (Ethiopian Version)
የአትክልት ላዛኛ

Just about everyone has their own version of a lasagna recipe. This is mine. See page 119 for a meat lasagna. (Can you tell I love cheese?)

Serves 4–6

- 2 pounds fresh spinach, washed and dried
- 2 medium red onions, diced
- ½ cup vegetable oil (or olive oil)
- 1 teaspoon grated ginger
- 4 cloves garlic, diced
- 1 (15-ounce) container ricotta cheese
- 2 cups grated cheddar cheese
- 4 cups grated mozzarella cheese
- 2 tablespoons fresh basil
- 2 tablespoons dried parsley
- 1 teaspoon dried oregano leaves
- 2 eggs
- Salt and pepper
- 1 teaspoon mitmita
- 1 box lasagna noodles
- 1 (24-ounce) jar marinara sauce
- ½ cup grated parmesan (optional)

Place the spinach in a medium pot and add enough water to cover it by 2 inches. Bring to a boil over high heat. Cook, stirring occasionally, until fully cooked, 10–15 minutes. Remove from the heat, drain, and let cool enough to touch. Roughly chop the spinach and set aside.

Place the onions and oil in a separate medium pot. Cook over medium heat until they are translucent and beginning to brown, about 5 minutes. Stir in the ginger and garlic and cook until just beginning to soften, about 4 minutes. Remove from the heat.

In a medium bowl, mix together the spinach, onion mixture, ricotta, cheddar, mozzarella, basil, parsley, oregano, eggs, salt and pepper to taste, and mitmita.

Cook the lasagna noodles according to package directions if needed. Preheat the oven to 350°F.

Spread one-third of the marinara sauce in a 9- × 13-inch lasagna dish. Add a layer of lasagna noodles, followed by one-third of the spinach and cheese sauce. Repeat the layering procedure until all the noodles are done. On the final layer, add the parmesan cheese (if using).

Cover the dish with aluminum foil and bake for 45 minutes. Uncover the dish and cook for an additional 15 minutes. The top of the lasagna will be browned and the marinara bubbling. If you're using the parmesan, the top will be browned and crispy. Remove from the heat and let cool for 10–15 minutes before eating.

Note: To make this vegan, simply use your favorite vegan cheese options for the cheeses.

የስጋ እና የአሳ ምግቦች

Meat & Fish Dishes

Ethiopian cuisine makes heavy use of various meats, and our meat dishes are frequently very spicy. Certain meat dishes are reserved for specific occasions, from casual gatherings and festivities to celebrations and holidays.

Others, like doro wot, are served at all occasions.

Doro Wot (Spicy Chicken Stew)

ዶሮ ወጥ

It doesn't get any more authentically Ethiopian than our national chicken dish. Doro wot is a slow-cooked spicy chicken stew that's served at every celebration and special event. You can't say you've truly tried Ethiopian food until you've tried this spicy and savory meal. Make sure to pair it with ergo (page 45) or ayib (page 41) if the heat is too much to handle! This is one of my all-time favorite dishes.

Serves 4–6

6 chicken drumsticks

Juice of 1 lemon

6 eggs

6 medium red (or yellow) onions, finely minced

1 cup oil (or ¼ cup kibe)

2 teaspoons grated ginger

6 cloves garlic, diced

1 cup berbere

4 cups water

1 tablespoon ground coriander

1 teaspoon ground cardamom

Salt and pepper

Remove the skin and fat from the drumsticks. Place the chicken in a medium bowl and add enough water to cover it by 3 inches. Mix in the lemon juice and leave the chicken to soak for 10 minutes. Drain and set aside.

Next, place the chicken in a medium pot and add enough water to cover it by 2 inches. Bring to a boil over medium heat and cook until rare to medium-rare but not fully cooked, 6–8 minutes. Remove from the heat, drain, and set aside.

Meanwhile, in a separate pot, add the eggs and enough water to cover them by 1 inch. Cover the pot and bring to a boil over medium heat. Boil until the eggs are hard-boiled, 10–15 minutes. Remove from the heat and drain. Place the eggs in a medium bowl and let cool enough to touch. Peel the eggs, rinse with water, and set aside.

In a large pot, add the onions and oil and cook on medium heat until the onions are translucent and beginning to brown, 8–10 minutes. Add the ginger and garlic, stir, and cook until just beginning to soften, about 4 minutes. Stir in the berbere and cook, stirring for about 2 minutes, making sure the powder does not clump. Add 4 cups of water and bring to a boil.

Add the chicken to the boiling sauce and stir. Turn down the heat to low, add the coriander, cardamom, and salt and pepper to taste, and stir. Cover and let cook, stirring occasionally, until the liquid is reduced and the sauce is moderately thick, 45 minutes–1 hour. Add the whole eggs and mix them well into the sauce. Cook for an additional 5 minutes, just to warm everything through and combine the flavors.

Serve hot with injera, rice, or your favorite whole grain bread.

Note: The milder version of this is called alicha doro wot (mild chicken stew) —የአልጫ ዶሮ ወጥ. Simply substitute the berbere with 2 teaspoons of turmeric and follow the same steps as above.

Ye Doro Wot Firfir (Chicken Sauce Firfir)

የዶሮ ወጥ ፍርፍር

Use up leftover doro wot with this quick and simple recipe.

2 cups doro wot

1 cup water

Salt

2 large injera (page 129, or ½ pound dirkosh)

Place the leftover doro wot in a medium pot and warm it through, stirring occasionally, on medium heat, about 10 minutes. Add the water and bring to a boil, still over medium heat. Add salt to taste, mix well, and remove from the heat.

Tear the large injera into bite-size pieces and add it in the pot. Mix well until the sauce is evenly distributed and has soaked into all the pieces of injera.

Serve hot with more injera, rice, or your favorite whole grain bread.

Asa Wot (Spicy Fish Stew)

የዓሣ ወጥ

This is a spicy fish stew that I especially enjoy during the winter months. Served on injera (page 129) or over rice, asa wot is perfect for non-meat eaters. It's a popular dish during Lent and other fasting periods.

Serves 4–6

2 medium yellow (or red) onions, thinly sliced

1/4 cup vegetable oil (or olive oil)

1 teaspoon grated ginger

5 cloves garlic, diced

2 tablespoons berbere

2 cups water

2 pounds white fish (cod, bass, or halibut all work well), cut into 2-inch cubes

4 jalapeños, deseeded and diced

Salt and pepper

Place the onions and oil in a medium pot. Cook over medium heat until the onions are translucent and beginning to brown, about 5 minutes. Add the ginger and garlic and stir until just beginning to soften, about 4 minutes. Stir in the berbere, making sure it does not clump, about 2 minutes. Add the water and bring to a boil, still over medium heat.

When the water is boiling, stir in the fish. Turn down the heat to low and stir in the jalapeños and salt and pepper to taste. Cover and let cook, stirring occasionally, until the liquid is reduced by about half and the sauce is moderately thick, 10–15 minutes.

Serve hot with injera, rice, or your favorite whole grain bread.

Kitfo (Ethiopian Beef Tartare)
ክትፎ

If you asked me what dish I would request for my last meal, my answer would be kitfo. This wholesome, spicy, flavorful dish is a staple in Ethiopian cuisine. I guarantee you have never had a tartare like this.

Serves 4–6

2 pounds grass-fed sirloin beef (or top round)

2 cups kibe

1 tablespoon ground cardamom

2 tablespoons mitmita

1 teaspoon salt

Cut any fat off the meat and then cut the meat into smaller pieces. Place it in a food processor fitted with a steel blade and pulse until you have ground beef. Transfer to a bowl and set aside.

In a medium pot, melt the kibe over low heat. As it melts, stir in the cardamom, mitmita, and salt. Remove from the heat and let rest for 2–3 minutes.

Slowly pour the kibe mixture over the meat, mixing constantly so the ingredients are evenly distributed. Continue to mix until the meat turns bright red, 10–15 minutes, and then let sit for 5 minutes before serving.

Serve with injera, rice, or your favorite whole grain bread.

Chicken Cotoletta (Ethiopian Chicken Schnitzel)

ኮቶሌት

It may not be listed on the menu, but chicken cotoletta is found at every Ethiopian restaurant. It is like a secret menu item and very popular among non-Ethiopian clients. Every household has their own version of this recipe. This is mine. If you're looking to spice it up a bit, serve it with a side of awaze (page 40).

Serves 4–6

1 pound boneless, skinless chicken breasts

Juice of 1 lemon

4 eggs

2 cloves garlic, diced

⅓ cup milk

2 tablespoons flat-leaf parsley, chopped

Salt and pepper

3 cups dried breadcrumbs

2 tablespoons grated parmesan cheese

1 tablespoon salted butter

1 cup olive oil (or vegetable oil)

Lemon wedges, for serving

Place the chicken in a medium bowl and add enough water to cover it by 3 inches. Mix in the lemon juice. Let the chicken soak for 10 minutes, then drain and pat dry. Next, halve the chicken breast horizontally and, using a meat mallet or a rolling pin, pound it until it is no more than ½-inch thick.

In a medium bowl, beat the eggs. Mix in the garlic and milk, followed by the parsley and salt and pepper to taste. In a separate bowl, mix together the breadcrumbs and parmesan.

Dip the chicken in the egg mixture, let any excess egg drip off, and then dip and fully coat it in the breadcrumb mixture. Pat well so the breadcrumbs adhere.

Melt the butter with the oil in a skillet over medium heat. Once the butter is fully melted and looks frothy, 5–7 minutes, cook the chicken pieces in batches until golden brown on both sides, about 5 minutes per side. Remove from the heat and place on paper towel to soak up any excess oil.

Sprinkle with a pinch of salt and serve hot with lemon wedges on the side.

Minchet Abish Wot (Spicy Ground Beef Stew)
የምንቸት አብሽ ወጥ

If a spicy, flavorful, and hearty dish is what you're looking for, look no further. This delicious authentic beef stew is quick and easy to make. It is traditionally served on holidays, at weddings, and at special events but can be enjoyed as an everyday meal. I think of it as a spicy Bolognese stew—Ethiopian-style.

Serves 4–6

3 medium yellow (or red) onions, diced

½ cup oil (or 2 tablespoons kibe)

1 teaspoons grated ginger

4 cloves garlic, diced

3 tablespoons berbere

1 cup water

1 pound lean ground beef

½ teaspoon ground cardamom

Salt

Place the onions and oil in a medium pot and cook over medium heat until the onions are translucent and beginning to brown, about 5 minutes. Add the ginger and garlic and cook, stirring, until just beginning to soften, about 4 minutes. Stir in the berbere, making sure it does not clump up. Add the water and bring to a boil.

Once the water is boiling, add the beef to the boiling sauce and mix well. Turn down the heat to low, add the cardamom and salt to taste, and stir. Cover and let cook, stirring occasionally, until the liquid is reduced by half and the sauce is moderately thick, 20–25 minutes.

Serve hot with injera, rice, or your favorite whole grain bread.

Note: The milder version of this dish is called ye minchet abish alicha wot (mild ground beef stew) — የምንቸት አብሽ አልጫ ወጥ. Simply substitute the berbere with 1 teaspoon of ground turmeric and follow the same steps as above.

Pasta al Forno (Ethiopian-Style One-Pot Pasta Dish)

ፓስታልፎርኖ

I have the fondest memories of my aunties making this dish when I was a child. This is another meal that shows the influence that Italian culture has on Ethiopia. It is a one-pot pasta dish that is easy to make and very popular as an alternative to our traditional dishes.

Serves 4–6

1 pound spaghetti

2 pounds ground beef chuck

1 medium yellow onion, diced

3 tablespoon vegetable oil (or olive oil)

1 teaspoons grated ginger

4 cloves garlic, diced

1 (28-ounce) can crushed tomatoes (or 1 [28-ounce] jar marinara sauce)

2 tablespoons tomato paste

1 cup water

1 sprig fresh rosemary (optional)

Salt and pepper

2 tablespoons unsalted butter

¼ cup all-purpose flour

1 cup whole milk

3 eggs, beaten

½–1 cup shredded mozzarella cheese

Cook the spaghetti to al dente (usually about 5 minutes less than the package directions say). Drain and set aside.

Place the beef in a medium pot and add enough water to cover it by 2 inches. Bring to a boil over medium heat and cook, stirring occasionally, until rare to medium-rare but not fully cooked. Remove from the heat, drain, and set aside.

Place the onions and oil in a large pot. Cook over medium heat until the onions are translucent and beginning to brown, about 5 minutes. Add the ginger and garlic and stir until just beginning to soften, about 4 minutes. Next, add the ground beef and cook, stirring occasionally, until fully cooked, 5 minutes.

Mix in the crushed tomatoes, tomato paste, and 1 cup of water and bring to a boil. Add the rosemary (if using) and salt and pepper to taste. Cook for another 5 minutes, just to warm everything through and combine the flavors. Remove from the heat, discard the rosemary (if used), and mix in the cooked spaghetti.

In a medium pan, melt the butter over medium heat. Add the flour, milk, and pepper to taste and bring to a boil, stirring continuously. When it reaches a boil, turn down the heat to a simmer and cook until the sauce thickens, 3–4 minutes. Remove from the heat and add to the pasta. Mix in the beaten eggs.

Preheat the oven to 350°F. Pour the pasta and sauce into a 9- × 13-inch baking pan. Sprinkle the mozzarella over top and bake, uncovered, until bubbling and browned on top, 25 minutes. Remove from the oven and let cool for 5–10 minutes before serving.

Enjoy with injera or your favorite whole grain bread or by itself.

Note: To make this dish vegetarian (but not vegan), simply omit the beef and replace it with the same weight of mushrooms or your favorite vegetables.

Siga Wot (Spicy Beef Stew)
የስጋ ወጥ

Simple and full of bold flavors and spices, siga wot sums up what Ethiopian cuisine is all about. I often serve it when I'm introducing friends to my cooking for the first time. It's a favorite of mine that satisfies my cravings for heat! Just make sure that you like spicy food first, as this is somewhere around Fire on the Taco Bell spice scale (see page 18).

Serves 4–6

- 2 pounds chuck roast cut beef (or bottom round roast), cut in 1- to 2-inch cubes
- 2 medium yellow onions, diced
- ¼ cup vegetable oil (or 2 tablespoons kibe)
- 1 teaspoons grated ginger
- 4 cloves garlic, diced
- 3 tablespoons berbere
- 2 cups water
- Salt and pepper

Place the beef in a medium pot and add enough water to cover it by 2 inches. Bring to a boil over medium heat and cook, stirring occasionally, until rare to medium-rare but not fully cooked. Remove from the heat, drain, and set aside.

Meanwhile, in a separate pot, add the onions and oil and cook over medium heat until the onions are translucent and beginning to brown, about 5 minutes. Add the ginger and garlic and cook, stirring, until just beginning to soften, about 4 minutes. Stir in the berbere, making sure it does not clump. Add 2 cups of water and bring to a boil.

Once the water is boiling, add the beef and stir. Turn down the heat to low, add salt and pepper to taste, and stir. Cover and let cook, stirring occasionally, until the liquid is reduced by half and the sauce is moderately thick, 20–25 minutes.

Serve with injera, rice, or your favorite whole grain bread.

Note: The milder version of this is called alicha siga wot (mild beef stew) — የሰጋ አልጫ ወጥ. Simply substitute the berbere with 1 teaspoon of turmeric and follow the steps above.

Ye Beg Alicha Wot (Mild Lamb Stew)
የበግ አልጫ ወጥ

One of my father's favorite dishes, ye beg alicha is a mild lamb stew traditionally served for Christmas, celebrations, and special events. When we were growing up, my brother and I used to compete for the largest leg of lamb and have the maids break it open for us. Then my dad would scoop out and feed us the delicious bone marrow. Ah, the good old days!

Serves 4–6

2 pounds lamb shoulder (or leg of lamb), cut into 1- to 2-inch cubes

2 large yellow onions, diced

½ cup oil (or 3 tablespoons kibe)

2 teaspoons grated ginger

4 cloves garlic, diced

1 teaspoon ground turmeric

2 cups water

1 tablespoon ground coriander

1 teaspoon ground cardamom

Salt

Place the lamb in a medium pot and add enough water to cover it by 2 inches. Bring to a boil over medium heat. Cook, stirring occasionally, until the lamb is rare to medium-rare but not fully cooked, about 5–8 minutes. Remove from the heat, drain, and set aside.

Meanwhile, add the onions and oil to a separate pot. Cook over medium heat until the onions are translucent and beginning to brown, about 5 minutes. Add the ginger and garlic and cook, stirring, until just beginning to soften, about 4 minutes. Stir in the turmeric, making sure it does not clump. Add 2 cups of water and bring to a boil.

Once the water is boiling, add the lamb to the boiling sauce and stir. Turn down the heat to low, add the coriander, cardamom, and salt to taste, and stir. Cover the pot and let cook, stirring occasionally, until the liquid is reduced by half and the sauce is moderately thick, 20–25 minutes.

Serve hot with injera, rice, or your favorite whole grain bread.

Note: The spicier version of this is called ye beg key wot (spicy lamb stew) — የበግ ቀይ ወጥ. Simply substitute the turmeric with ¼ cup of berbere and follow the steps above.

Ye Beg Kikil (Lamb Broth Stew)
የበግ ቅቅል

My niece and nephew love this dish! My mom makes it almost every weekend for them, and it's their special time with Grandma. It's so sweet to watch them create amazing memories around food, the way I've been so blessed to do.

Serves 4–6

5 pounds lamb shoulder (or shoulder blade chops), bone-in, trimmed of excess fat

2 pounds lamb shoulder (or leg of lamb), cut in 1- to 2-inch cubes

5 medium yellow (or red) onions, diced

1 cup vegetable oil (or ¾ cup kibe)

3 large leeks, thinly sliced into rounds

4 cups water, divided

4 cloves garlic, diced

2 teaspoons grated ginger

1 teaspoon ground turmeric

8 jalapeño peppers, deseeded and diced (optional)

1 sprig rosemary (optional)

Salt

Place all the lamb meat in a medium pot and add enough water to cover it by 2 inches. Bring to a boil over medium heat. Cook, stirring occasionally, until the lamb is rare to medium-rare but not fully cooked, about 5–8 minutes. Remove from the heat, drain, and set aside.

Place the onions and oil in a separate medium pot. Cook over medium heat until the onions are translucent and beginning to brown, about 5 minutes. Mix in the lamb meat, leeks, and 1 cup of the water. Cook over medium heat, stirring occasionally, until the water begins to boil, about 5 minutes.

Stir in the garlic, ginger, and turmeric, making sure the powder does not clump. Stir and cook until the garlic just begins to soften, about 4 minutes. Add the remaining 3 cups of water and bring to a boil. Turn down the heat to low and stir in the jalapeños and rosemary (if using) and salt to taste. Cover and cook, stirring occasionally, until the meat is fully cooked and falling off the bone, about 20 minutes.

Serve hot with injera, rice, or your favorite whole grain bread.

Note: Another way to serve this dish is by making fitfit (see page 20) with it: Tear 1–2 large injera (page 129) into bite-size pieces and place them in a medium bowl. Pour the lamb broth and meat over top and mix well until the sauce is evenly distributed and has soaked into all the pieces of injera. Serve hot with more injera, rice, or your favorite whole grain bread.

Tibs (Beef Stir-Fry)
ጥብስ

Tibs is an Ethiopian dish that consists of stir-fried meat. I think of it as being a very masculine dish. My dad used to make it for us kids when our mom was away. Like a lot of Ethiopian men, he really liked spicy food! He used to eat raw jalapeños or serranos with all his meals and, being a daddy's girl, I started doing the same. Be sure to sear the beef on all sides before adding the other ingredients, and remember that it's not all about heat—the rosemary at the end gives this recipe an aromatic note too.

Serves 4–6

2 pounds chuck roast beef (or any lean beef), cut into 1- to 2-inch cubes

3 tablespoons oil (or 1 tablespoon kibe)

1 medium yellow onion, thinly sliced

3 cloves garlic, diced

1 tablespoon berbere

2 medium jalapeños, deseeded and thinly sliced

1 beefsteak tomato (or 2 Roma tomatoes), with their seeds, thinly sliced

1 sprig fresh rosemary (optional)

Salt and pepper

In a large non-stick skillet, sear the beef on all sides over medium-high heat, about 5 minutes in total. Add the oil, followed by the onions and garlic, and mix to combine. Let cook, stirring occasionally, until the onions and garlic begin to soften, 4–5 minutes.

Mix in the berbere, jalapeños, and tomatoes. Let cook for another 5 minutes, just to soften the tomatoes. Add the rosemary (if using) and salt and pepper to taste. Cover the skillet, turn down the heat to low, and let simmer, stirring occasionally, for 10–15 minutes, just to warm everything through and combine all the flavors.

Serve hot with injera, rice, or your favorite whole grain bread.

Notes:

To make fiyel tibs (goat stir-fry) — የፍየል ጥብስ, replace the beef with 2 pounds of goat meat cut in 1- to 2-inch cubes, omit the tomato, and follow the steps above.

To make ye beg tibs (lamb stir-fry) — የበግ ጥብስ, replace the beef with 2 pounds of lamb shoulder or leg of lamb, cut in 1- to 2-inch cubes. Omit the tomato, use 5 tablespoons of oil instead of 3 tablespoons (or 2 tablespoons of kibe, if you prefer), and follow the steps above.

To make doro tibs (chicken stir-fry) — የዶሮ ጥብስ, replace the beef with 1 pound of boneless, skinless chicken breast, cut in 1- to 2- inch cubes, and follow the steps above.

To make zilzil siga tibs (sautéed beef strips) — ዝልዝል ጥብስ, use the same cut of beef but cut it in long thin strips instead of cubes. Use 5 tablespoons of oil instead of 3 tablespoons (or 3 tablespoons of kibe instead of 1 tablespoon). Omit the tomato, use 3 jalapeños instead of 2, and follow the steps above.

Awaze Tibs (Extra-Spicy Beef Stir-Fry)
የአዋዜ ስጋ ጥብስ

This beef stir-fry is my go-to dish to make after work. Delicious, spicy, and flavorful, awaze tibs works great for any meal or occasion. For those of you who do not like saucy and spicy dishes, try derek tibs (dry stir-fry) for a great alternative (see note).

Serves 4–6

2 pounds chuck roast cut beef (or any lean beef), cut in 1- to 2-inch cubes

1 medium yellow onion, thinly sliced

3 cloves garlic, diced

3 tablespoons oil

2 medium jalapeños, deseeded and thinly sliced

1 red beefsteak tomato (or 2 Roma tomatoes), with their seeds, thinly sliced

1 cup awaze (page 40)

Salt and pepper

1 sprig fresh rosemary (optional)

In a large skillet over medium-high heat, cook the beef on all sides until it starts to brown, 4–5 minutes. Mix in the onions, garlic, and oil. Let cook, stirring constantly, until all the meat is fully browned, 8–10 minutes.

Mix in the jalapeños and tomatoes, stir, and let cook for 2 minutes, just to soften the jalapeños and tomatoes. Add the awaze, salt and pepper to taste, and rosemary (if using) and stir. Cover the skillet, turn down the heat to low, and simmer, stirring occasionally, for about 10 minutes, just to warm everything through and combine the flavors.

Remove from the heat and serve hot with injera, rice, or your favorite whole grain bread.

Note: To make derek tibs (dry beef stir-fry) — ደረቅ ጥብስ, omit the awaze and the tomato and use 3 jalapeños. Follow the instructions in paragraph 1, above, then add the jalapeños, salt and pepper to taste, and rosemary (if using), and mix well. Turn down the heat, cover, and let simmer, stirring occasionally, until the beef is cooked through and the gravy is reduced and thick, 5–10 minutes. Remove from the heat and serve hot with injera, rice, or your favorite whole grain bread.

Asa Tibs (Ethiopian Fried Fish)
ዓሳ ጥብስ

Although Ethiopian food is a very meat-forward cuisine, we use asa tibs as an easy substitute for meat equivalents. Popular during Lent, this dish is sure to please any pescatarian or anyone looking to eat healthier and lighter meals.

Serves 4–6

- 2 pounds white fish (cod, bass, or snapper all work well)
- 1 tablespoon berbere
- 5 tablespoons vegetable oil (or olive oil)
- Salt and pepper
- 1 medium yellow (or red) onion, thinly sliced
- 4 cloves garlic, diced
- 1 teaspoon grated ginger
- 3 jalapeños, deseeded and diced
- 1 lime, cut into wedges

Chop the fish into 1-inch cubes and place it in a container. Season with the berbere and let marinate in the refrigerator for a minimum of 15 minutes, or up to 1 hour for best results.

Warm the oil in a medium skillet over high heat. Fry the fish on both sides until crispy and golden brown, 5–6 minutes per side. Remove from the heat and set aside on paper towel to absorb any excess oil. Season with salt and pepper to taste.

Reduce the oil in the pan to 2–3 tablespoons, turn down the heat to medium, and add the onions, garlic, and ginger. Cook, stirring constantly, until the onions are translucent and beginning to brown, about 5 minutes. Add the jalapeños and stir for 4 more minutes, just to soften them a little.

Return the fish to the pan, squeeze one of the lime wedges over top, stir to combine, and sauté for 1 minute.

Remove from the heat and serve hot with the remaining lime wedges and injera, rice, or your favorite whole grain bread.

Gored Gored Tibs (Cubed Lean Beef)
ጎረድ ጎረድ

Who doesn't love a well-seasoned rare beef dish? This is similar to kitfo (page 99), but uses cubed beef instead of minced. A very popular national dish, gored gored is an easy simple meal that I enjoy with awaze (page 40) or mitmita to add an extra kick. Just talking about it makes my mouth water!

Serves 4–6

- 4 tablespoons oil (or 3 tablespoons kibe)
- 2 pounds tender high-end cut beef (ideally tenderloin), cut in 1- to 2-inch cubes
- 4 tablespoons berbere
- Salt and pepper

Warm the oil (or melt the kibe) in a large skillet over low heat. Add the beef and berbere and mix well. Cook, stirring constantly, until the meat is at your preferred temperature, 2–3 minutes. Traditionally it is served rare to medium-rare, which is what I recommend.

Remove from the heat and serve warm with injera, rice, or your favorite whole grain bread.

Meat Lasagna (Ethiopian Version)
የስጋ ላዛኛ

Very popular among my friend group and requested at every potluck I attend, this is my version of meat lasagna.

Serves 4–6

2 pounds lean ground beef

2 medium red (or yellow) onions, diced

⅔ cups vegetable oil (or olive oil)

1 teaspoons grated ginger

4 cloves garlic, diced

2 large tomatoes (Roma work well), with their seeds, diced

1 (15-ounce) can tomato sauce

1 tablespoon tomato paste

2 tablespoons fresh basil

2 tablespoons dried parsley

1 teaspoon dried oregano leaves

2 cups water

1 tablespoon berbere

Salt and pepper

1 box of lasagna noodles

1 (15-ounce) container ricotta cheese

2 cups grated cheddar cheese

4 cups grated mozzarella cheese

½ cup grated parmesan cheese (optional)

Place the beef in a medium pot and add enough water to cover it by 2 inches. Bring to a boil over medium heat and cook, stirring occasionally, until rare to medium-rare but not fully cooked. Remove from the heat, drain, and set aside.

Add the onions and oil to a medium pot. Cook over medium heat until the onions are translucent and beginning to brown, about 5 minutes. Stir in the ginger and garlic and cook until just beginning to soften, about 4 minutes.

Mix in the ground beef and cook, stirring occasionally, until fully cooked, about 5 minutes. Add the tomatoes, tomato sauce, and tomato paste and mix well again. Cook until the tomatoes just begin to soften, about 4 minutes. Mix in the basil, parsley, oregano, and 2 cups of water. Bring the sauce to a boil, stirring continuously.

When it reaches a boil, stir in the berbere and salt and pepper to taste. Cover, turn down the heat to low, and cook, stirring occasionally, until the liquid is reduced by one-third and the sauce is thick, about 15 minutes. Remove from the heat and set aside. Cook the lasagna noodles according to package directions if needed.

Spread one cup of the meat sauce in a 9- × 15-inch lasagna pan. Add a layer of lasagna noodles, followed by a layer of the meat sauce and then a layer of each of the cheeses (ricotta, cheddar, and mozzarella). Repeat the layering procedure until all the noodles are done. On the final layer, add the meat sauce and the parmesan (if using).

Preheat the oven to 375°F. Cover the dish with aluminum foil and bake for 1 hour. Uncover the dish and cook for an additional 15 minutes. The top of the lasagna will be browned and the sauce bubbling. If you're using the parmesan, the top will be browned and crispy.

Remove from the heat and let cool for 10–15 minutes before serving.

PHOTO GEO
Cunningham Street No
13 DEC 1958

Asa (Ethiopian Whole Fish)

ሙሉ ዓሣ ጥብስ

Who doesn't love a whole fish fried? This is my sister's favorite dish and one that conjures up some very fond memories for me. My uncle used to take me to a huge open-air marketplace called Merkato in Addis. It had a cafeteria-type spot right in the middle where the only thing on the menu was asa served with injera or bread. I can't make this dish and not think of him and the fun times we shared together.

Serves 4–6

1½–2 pounds whole fish, cleaned and descaled (red snapper or branzino work well)

1 cup oil

Salt and pepper

2 lemon wedges

Rinse and pat dry the fish. Using a sharp knife, score it by cutting about three or four horizontal slits about 1 inch apart on both sides of the fish. You just need to cut through the skin, not all the way through the whole fish.

In a medium pan large enough to hold the fish (the fish will probably be around 24 inches long), warm the oil over high heat. While the fish is cooking, use a large spoon to baste it periodically with the hot oil. Fry the fish until it is crispy and golden brown on both sides, 5–8 minutes per side. Remove from the heat and place on paper towel or parchment paper to drain off any excess oil.

Sprinkle with salt and pepper to taste and serve hot with lemon wedges on the side and injera, rice, or your favorite whole grain bread.

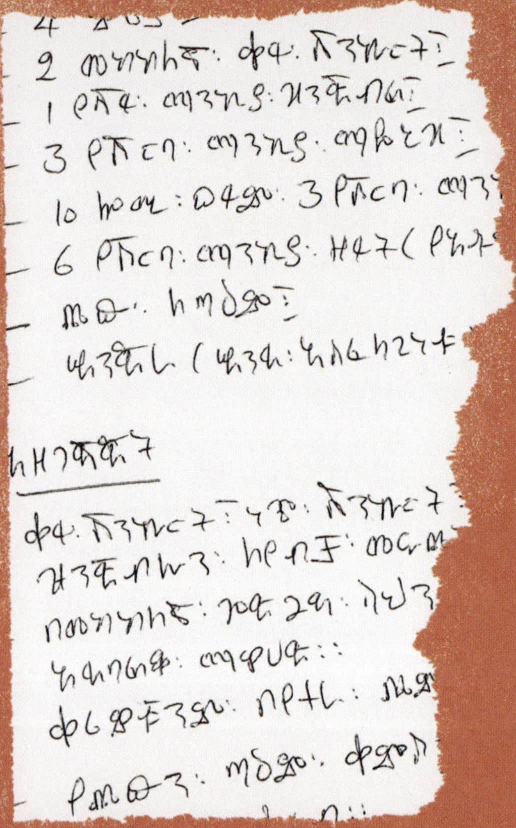

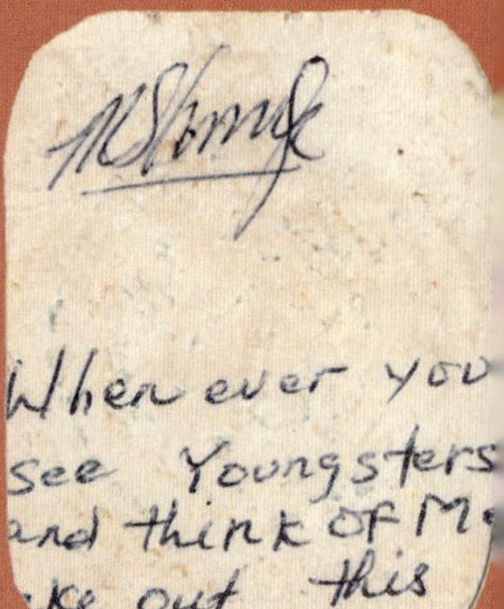

When ever you
see Youngsters
and think of M
ke out this

መክሰስ

Breads & Desserts

Injera, a soft, spongy sour flatbread, is arguably the most important part of Ethiopian cuisine—and it's possibly the most famous. It is the literal base for most meals. Meats, vegetables, and stews are served on top of a large round piece of injera that diners tear off piece by piece to be used as a sort of edible utensil.

Sweets and sugary foods are not common in traditional Ethiopian cuisine. Most Ethiopian desserts have a strong Western influence—Italian, in particular.

Injera (Ethiopian Sour Flatbread)
እንጀራ

You can't eat Ethiopian food without injera. It's the tortilla to the taco, the peanut butter to the jelly, and the milk to the cereal. We traditionally eat with our hands, using this staple flatbread to scoop up our meals. Its sour, spongy flavor pairs well with the traditional spicy wots and balances out all of the flavors. Traditionally made with teff flour, injera is the staple of Ethiopian cuisine.

Serves 4–6

Starter

1 cup teff

1 cup warm water (hand-hot)

¼ teaspoon rapid rise instant yeast

Dough

6 cups teff

1 teaspoon ground fenugreek seed

2 cups warm water (hand-hot)

Sparkling water (optional)

To prepare the starter, mix the teff with the water in a medium bowl and sprinkle the yeast over top. Mix well, cover tightly with plastic wrap to seal, and set aside at room temperature for 3 days to ferment.

After 3 days, the starter and water will separate. Pour off the water that is floating on top. This step is crucial for success.

To prepare the dough, mix the teff and fenugreek with the water and your dough starter. Mix well, adding warm water as needed, about 1 tablespoon at a time, until the batter is smooth and liquid, similar to a pancake batter. Cover tightly with plastic wrap to seal, and set aside at room temperature for 24 hours to ferment.

After 24 hours, the batter is ready to be cooked. Pour off any water floating on top. If the batter is too thick, add unflavored sparkling water (preferably Perrier), about 1 tablespoon at a time, and mix well until the batter is light and liquid.

Heat a mitad (see page 9) to 250°F. If you don't have a mitad, you can use a non-stick stove-top pan or griddle over medium heat. Coat the surface of the mitad or pan with a thin layer of the injera batter. It should be thicker than a crepe but thinner than a pancake. Try adding 1 cup of batter to see how that works in your pan and then adjust as required. Cook until you see bubbles start to form and let them pop, 3–5 minutes. Cover the mitad or pan with a lid and let the steam cook the injera for a couple more minutes until the batter is fully cooked through. Remove the injera and repeat with the remaining batter.

Enjoy with any traditional Ethiopian wots.

Notes:

To turn your injera into a spicy snack, try making kategna (spicy flatbread) — ቃተኛ: In a small bowl, mix 2 tablespoons of melted kibe with 1 tablespoon of berbere until you have a smooth consistency. Spread it on fresh injera or warmed-up day-old injera.

Injera can be stored in a *messob* (injera storage unit) or on a plate and covered with a lid at room temperature or in the fridge for up to 7 days.

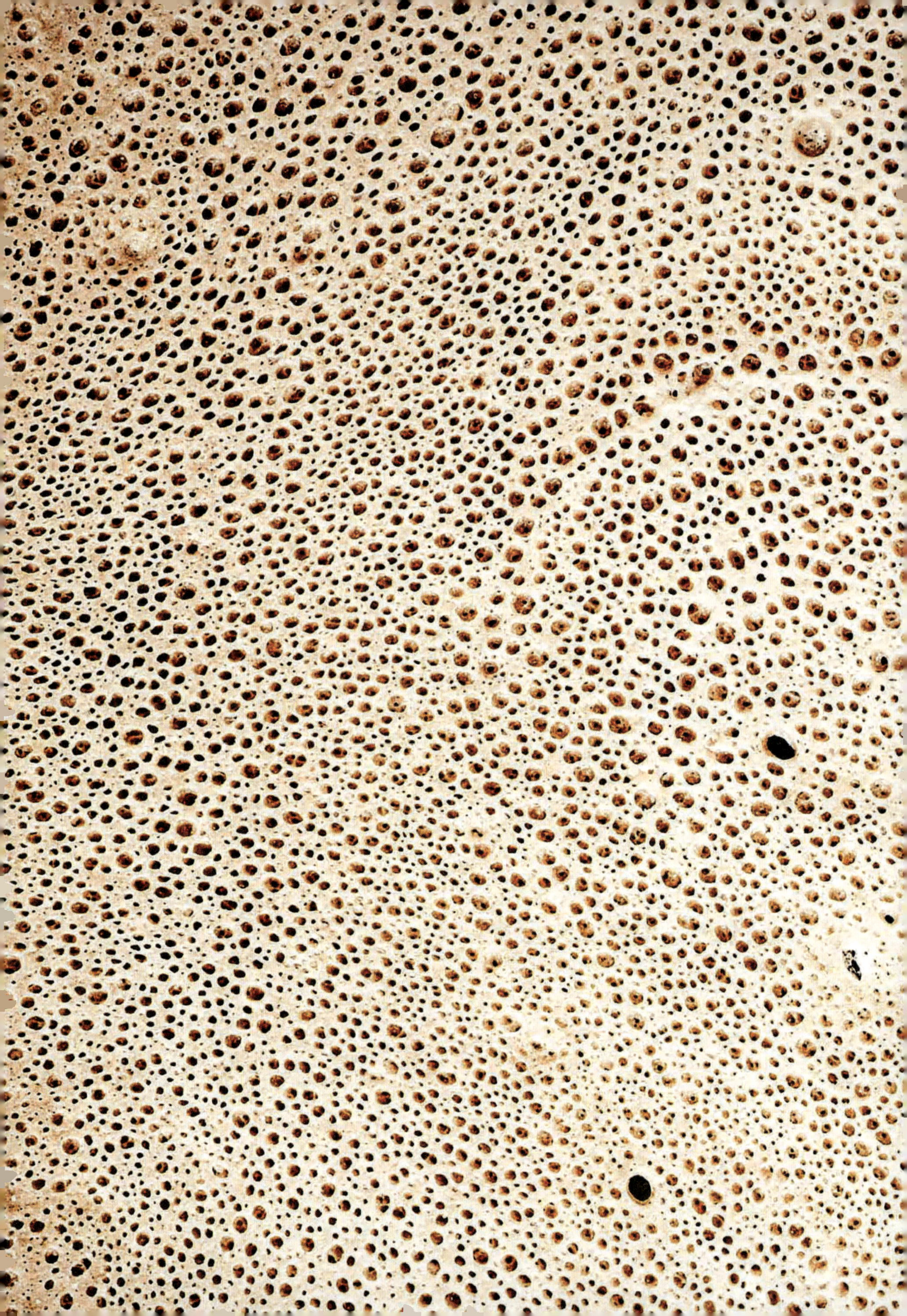

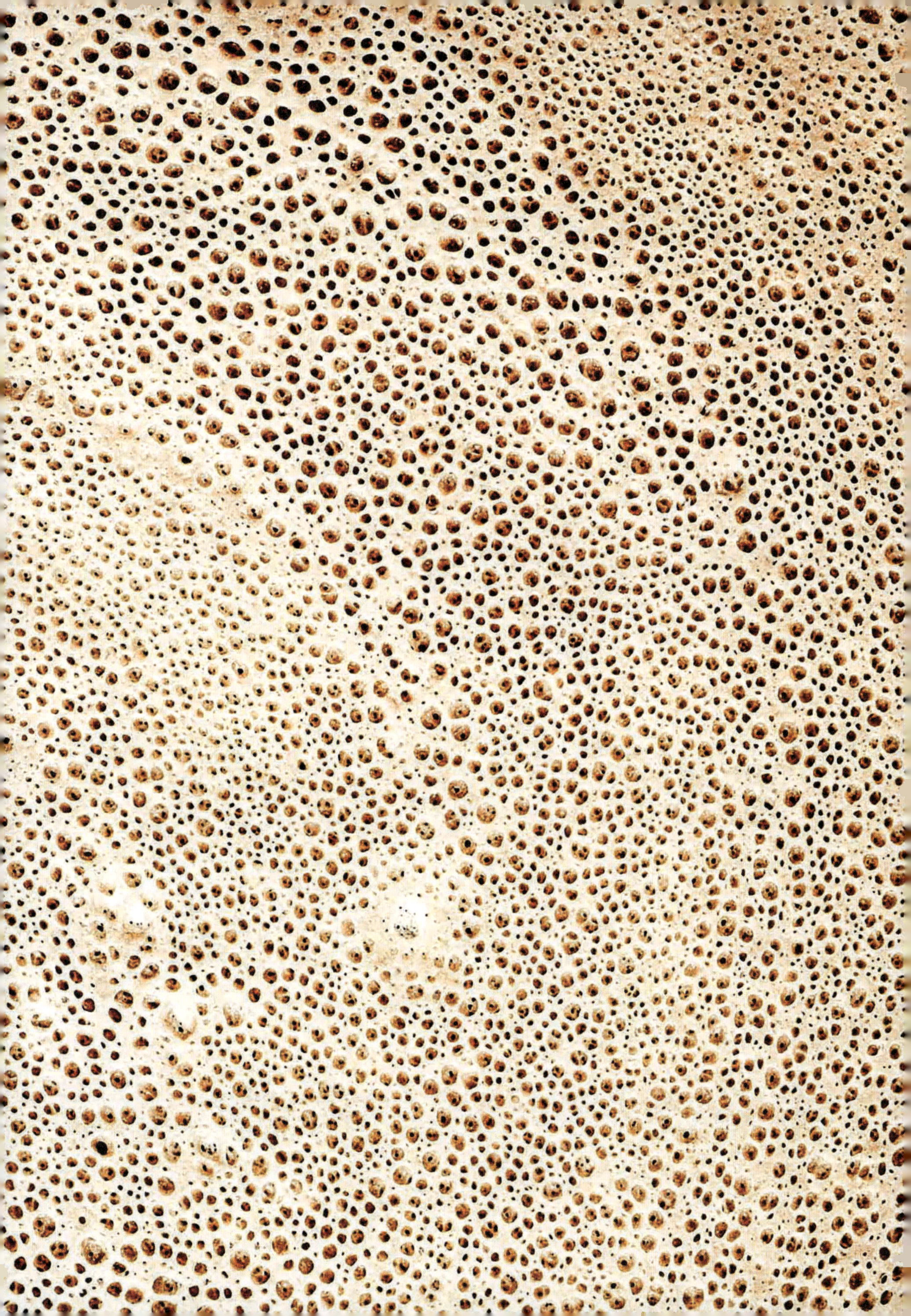

Ambasha (Ethiopian Traditional Bread)
አምባሻ

Every celebration and event calls for ambasha. There are various ways to prepare it, and this is the one that my auntie taught me. I used to love sitting next to her in the kitchen, fork at the ready, so I could create its beautiful wheel-like pattern. I even used to try to write my name in it in tiny print. This celebratory bread is semi-sweet and goes so well with our traditional coffee ceremony (page 147). It can be stored in an airtight container at room temperature for up to 5 days.

Makes one 12-inch loaf

4 cups warm water (hand-hot), divided

¼ cup rapid rise instant yeast

1 teaspoon baking powder

1 teaspoon salt

2 eggs

½ cup olive oil, divided

6 cups all-purpose flour

¼ cup granulated sugar

1 tablespoon tikur azmud

In a medium bowl, mix 1 cup of the water with the yeast. Whisk in the baking powder, salt, eggs, and ¼ cup of the oil until the mixture is lump-free. Let sit, covered, at room temperature for 1 hour.

Place the flour, sugar, and tikur azmud in a large bowl and, stirring constantly, slowly pour in the yeast mixture. Gradually mix in the rest of the warm water as needed, about ¼ cup at a time, until the batter is smooth and thick, very similar to bread dough. Mix well, cover tightly with plastic wrap to seal, and set aside at room temperature until the dough doubles in size, 1–2 hours.

Next, put the dough on a lightly floured work surface and flatten it into a circle about 12 inches in diameter. Using a table knife, mark seven or eight concentric circles on the dough, working from the center to the edges, then make cuts intersecting in the center to form a wheel pattern. You only want to mark the surface of the dough. Don't cut too deep. Rub some olive oil on your hands, work surface, and knife if the dough sticks to any of them.

Heat a mitad (see page 9) to 350°F. If you don't have a mitad, you can use a stove-top griddle over medium heat. Coat the surface of the mitad or griddle with a thin layer of olive oil. Place the dough on the mitad, with the design side facing up, and cook until and the underside is golden brown, about 10 minutes. Flip and cook on the other side until fully cooked and browned, about 10 minutes. Remove from the heat, let cool enough to touch, then lightly brush with olive oil before enjoying with a traditional Ethiopian coffee or your favorite beverage.

Defo Dabo (Ethiopian Bread)
ድፎ ዳቦ

This is more of our daily bread, but it is also served on celebratory occasions. My dad loved eating this bread every morning with margarine and a cup of coffee or tosign tea (page 149). Every time I bake this, I go back to those mornings sitting next to him and listening to him tell a story or a joke in between bites. This will keep in a bread box at room temperature for up to 2 days.

Serves 4–6

- 8 cups warm water (hand-hot), divided
- 1 tablespoon rapid rise instant yeast
- 6 cups all-purpose flour
- 1 tablespoon white peppercorns
- 1 tablespoon vanilla extract
- ¼ cup olive oil
- 1 teaspoon salt
- 1 tablespoon tikur azmud

In a medium bowl, mix ⅔ cup of the water with the yeast. Let sit, covered, at room temperature for 30 minutes to ferment.

In a separate medium bowl, mix together the yeast-water, flour, peppercorns, vanilla, olive oil, and salt. Gradually add the remaining water as needed, about ½ cup at a time, until the dough is thick, very similar to bread dough, and lump-free.

Mix in the tikur azmud. Cover the bowl with plastic wrap and let sit at room temperature until the dough doubles in size, about 30 minutes.

Preheat the oven to 425°F.

Place the dough on a baking tray and bake until golden brown, 45 minutes–1 hour.

Let cool on a wire rack for 5–10 minutes before slicing and enjoying with a traditional Ethiopian coffee or your favorite beverage.

Kita (Ethiopian Spicy Flatbread)
ቂጣ

An authentic Ethiopian flatbread, kita, sometimes spelled kitta, is made from the simplest ingredients but packs a bold, savory flavor. When I was a child I used to call it the Ethiopian pancake, which always made my uncle laugh. He then started calling it the same thing. When I went home to visit as an adult, on my first morning there we went to a restaurant and he looked at me and said, "Would you like an Ethiopian pancake for breakfast?" We both started laughing. The server was confused, but I will forever cherish this joke we share.

Serves 4–6

- 2 cups bread flour
- 1 teaspoon salt
- 1 cup warm water (hand-hot)
- 2 tablespoons kibe (or 4 tablespoons olive oil)
- 1 tablespoon berbere

In a medium bowl, mix together the flour, salt, and water. Once the batter is thick enough to coat the back of a spoon and lump-free, it is ready to use.

Heat a mitad (see page 9) to 250°F. If you don't have a mitad, you can use a stove-top griddle over medium heat. Coat the surface of the mitad or griddle with a semi-thin layer of batter. It should be about as thick as a layer of pancake batter. Cook until the underside is golden brown, about 5 minutes, and then flip to cook the other side until golden brown, about 5 minutes. Remove from the heat and set aside.

In a small bowl, mix together the kibe, berbere, and salt to taste. Once you have a smooth consistency, spread it all over one side of the warm kita and enjoy!

Kita is best eaten the day it's made, but you can use up leftovers in chechebsa (page 55). You can make chechebsa with as little as two slices of kita. Use 2–3 tablespoons of oil and 1–2 teaspoons of berbere for every 2 kitas.

Baklava (Ethiopian Version)
ባቅላቫ

This dessert is a staple in Ethiopian cuisine. It is not an authentic or traditional Ethiopian dessert, but it's one that we enjoy regularly. This sweet pastry is popular in many other cultures as well and is a favorite among Habeshas, descendants of people with ethnic connections to Abyssinia, modern-day Ethiopia and Eritrea. With its layers of phyllo dough, nuts, and honey, I think of this dish as a sweet lasagna. Leftovers will keep in an airtight container at room temperature for 1–2 days.

Serves 4–6

- 2 cups unsalted chopped nuts (walnuts, almonds, pistachios, or hazelnuts)
- 2 teaspoons ground cinnamon
- 1 (16-ounce) packet phyllo dough, thawed
- 1 cup unsalted butter, melted
- 1 cup water
- 1 tablespoon lemon juice
- 1 cup sugar
- 1 cinnamon stick
- ½ cup honey
- ½ teaspoon vanilla extract
- 1 teaspoon grated orange zest
- Finely chopped pistachios, for garnish

Preheat the oven to 350°F. Lightly grease the bottom and sides of a 9- × 13-inch baking pan.

In a medium bowl, mix together the chopped nuts and cinnamon. Scoop out 1–2 tablespoons of the nuts and pat them onto the sides of the baking pan, all the way to the top.

Working with one sheet of phyllo at a time, and keeping the remainder covered, brush each sheet with the melted butter and then place it in the baking pan. For every 5 sheets of phyllo you place in the pan, sprinkle 3 tablespoons of the nuts and cinnamon mixture evenly over top. Continue in this way until you've used all the phyllo, ending with the phyllo dough on top.

Using a very sharp knife, cut the baklava into diamond shapes. Bake, uncovered, until crisp and golden brown, 40–45 minutes.

At the 30-minute point, make the sauce. In a small pot, mix together the water, lemon juice, sugar, and cinnamon stick and bring to a boil over medium-high heat. Stir in the honey, vanilla, and orange zest and turn down the heat to low. Cook, stirring occasionally, until slightly thickened, about 10 minutes. Remove from the heat, discard the cinnamon stick, and set the sauce aside to cool.

Once the baklava is golden brown, 40–45 minutes, remove from the oven and immediately spoon the cooled sauce evenly over top. Let it sit, uncovered, at room temperature (do not refrigerate) for a minimum of 4 hours, or overnight for best results.

Garnish with finely chopped pistachios and enjoy with a cup of Ethiopian coffee or your favorite beverage.

Milifoli (Ethiopian Millefoglie Cake)
ሚሊፎሊ

Here is one of my favorite desserts by far. Milifoli, sometimes pronounced "milifoni" by Ethiopians, is the dessert of my childhood. I have so many special memories of trips to Enrico, a popular café in Addis, with my father and my auntie, where I devoured several of these heavenly cakes in a single sitting. Now I make them at home and each bite transports me back to those special days that I miss so much. Leftovers can be stored in an airtight container in the fridge for up to 3 days.

Serves 4–6

2 cups whole milk

1 cup heavy (30%–36%) cream

3 eggs

½ cup granulated sugar

¼ cup corn starch

2 tablespoons unsalted butter

1 teaspoon pure vanilla extract

1 (17.3-ounce) package puff pastry dough (2 sheets), thawed

Icing sugar for baking and decorating

Mix the milk and cream together in a medium pot. Add the eggs, sugar, and corn starch and mix again. Place the pot over medium heat and, stirring continuously, warm the mixture until it is thick, creamy, and lump-free, 7–9 minutes.

Add the butter and vanilla and continue to mix until the butter is fully melted and the mixture has a smooth consistency. Remove from the heat and place in a medium bowl. Cover and refrigerate for a minimum of 1 hour, or up to overnight.

Preheat the oven to 375°F.

Unroll the puff pastry sheets onto the parchment paper they were wrapped in and lightly dust all over with icing sugar. Prick each sheet all over with a fork to make small holes in the dough to let it breathe while baking and prevent it from rising too much.

Transfer the pastry, still on the parchment, to baking sheets and bake until light golden brown, 10–15 minutes. Remove from the oven, let cool enough to touch, then cut each sheet lengthwise into three.

To assemble: In a serving tray, place a layer of cooked pastry and spread an even layer of the cream mixture on top. Place another sheet of pastry on top and repeat the process with the second layer. Cover with another pastry sheet, add a third and final layer of cream and dust with the powdered sugar.

Cut the cake into small, equally sized rectangles and enjoy with a traditional Ethiopian coffee or your favorite beverage.

Welcome to Dallas

Tiramisu

ቲራሚሱ

Another popular dessert in Ethiopian cuisine is tiramisu. This is another dish from the Western world we have adopted into our cuisine. While there are many different variations of this recipe, this simple and easy version is the one I enjoy the most. Sometimes keeping it simple is the best way!

Serves 4–6

- 2 cups heavy (30%–36%) cream
- ⅓ cup sugar
- 1 cup mascarpone cheese, at room temperature
- 1 teaspoon vanilla extract
- 2 cups cold espresso (ideally Ethiopian coffee)
- 1 tablespoon amaretto or Kahlúa (optional)
- ½ (17.6ounce) package lady fingers (sponge fingers) or 32 pieces of ladyfingers
- 2 tablespoons cocoa powder

In a medium bowl, use a handheld or electric mixer to whip the cream and sugar until smooth and stiff. Add the mascarpone cheese and vanilla, and whip again until the mixture is stiff and peaks form. Set aside.

In a separate bowl, wide enough to hold a lady finger, place the coffee and amaretto (if using) and mix. Quickly dip the lady fingers in the coffee, without letting them soak, and place them in a 9- × 11-inch baking pan (no need to grease or line the pan) in a single layer.

Using a spatula, spread half of the cream mixture on top of the lady fingers. Place another layer of coffee-dipped lady fingers on top of the cream, cover with another layer of the cream mixture, and dust generously with cocoa powder. Refrigerate, uncovered, for a minimum 30 minutes, or up to overnight (I find 3–4 hours gives the best results).

Enjoy with a traditional Ethiopian coffee or your favorite beverage.

መጠጠች

Beverages

Coffee is extremely important in Ethiopian cuisine and culture. We even have a coffee ceremony which is not specific to any holiday or occasion but is performed as a daily routine.

Coffee was first discovered in Ethiopia by a goat herder. Legend says that the goats started eating berries from a certain tree and became extremely energetic afterward. The goat herder told his local priest what had happened and the priest made a drink out of the berries, to help him stay up all night for his long overnight prayers. When the priest saw how well it worked, he started sharing it among other priests. The news started to spread and now coffee is enjoyed all over the world.

Another popular beverage is tej, which is a homemade honey wine unique to Ethiopian cuisine. This popular beverage is served during any celebration or special occasion and is served in *tej bet*, or "honey wine houses."

Buna (Ethiopian Traditional Coffee Ceremony)
ቡና

When I say ceremony, I mean it. There is no "let's just pour a cup of coffee and run"—it takes time, and there are steps and procedures to follow. Setting up for a proper Ethiopian coffee ceremony involves a *jebena* (coffee pot), *sini* (coffee cups), *ye buna mintaf* (carpet to be placed on the ground), *rekebot* (serving tray), spoons, and *etan machesha* (incense stand). This coffee ceremony is performed two or three times every single day. It is our way of enjoying each other's company, taking time to talk and catch up and have a break from the everyday hustle and bustle. But be aware, this is not your normal cup of joe. It is very concentrated and strong—and sure to wake you up!

Makes 4 cups

½ cup raw Ethiopian coffee beans

4 cups water

Wash the coffee beans in cold or room-temperature water. Next, in a medium pan, place the beans over medium heat (you don't need to dry the beans before you do this). Roast, stirring occasionally, until all the beans are fully cooked and black, 6–7 minutes. Remove from the heat and set aside on a plate or in a bowl.

Once the beans are cool enough to touch, grind them in a *mefcha* (Ethiopian mortar and pestle) or a coffee grinder until fully turned into powder.

Pour 4 cups of water into the jebena, bring to a boil over low heat, and keep at a boil for 5 minutes. Add the coffee and bring back to a boil over low heat again. Once the coffee boils, remove from the heat and set aside on the base of the jebena for 5 minutes (letting the coffee grinds settle on the bottom). Serve in the sini and repeat the step for total of three rounds of coffee. The first round is called abol or the first cup of coffee.

Serve with popcorn or your favorite Ethiopian snack (pages 29–45) or dessert (pages 133–141).

Note: The second and third rounds of coffee are called *huletegna* (second) and *sostegna* (third).

Kuti (Ethiopian Tea & Coffee Blend)

ቁጢ

This mildly caffeinated beverage is a blend of coffee and tea. It originates from the Harar region, in northwest Ethiopia, which is where my father is from. The first time I had it was when I went with my father on a business trip to Diredawa. I was apprehensive at first, but after trying it, I was a convert and quickly understood why it is so popular.

Makes 4 cups

½ pound dry coffee leaves

4 cups water

1 teaspoon tea spices (see Notes)

In a medium skillet, fry the coffee leaves on low heat until fragrant, about 3 minutes. Remove from the heat and transfer to your tea pot.

Next, put the water in a tea kettle (or pot), add the coffee leaves and tea spices, and bring to a boil over medium heat. Once the water is fully boiled, remove from the heat and let stand for 5 minutes.

Enjoy with your favorite Ethiopian snack (pages 29–45) or by itself!

Notes:

I buy a ready-made mix that contains cinnamon, cardamom, and cloves. Chai spice mix is a good substitute.

It's important to boil the coffee leaves and tea spices with the water, rather than boiling water and pouring it over top of them.

Tosign Tea (Thyme Tea)
የጦስኝ ሻይ

This is not your average thyme tea. The thyme grows in the fertile lands of Ethiopia and is 100% organic. After harvesting it is normally sun-dried and sold in the open markets. The blend of spices and herbs smell amazing and remind me of the rainy season when I was growing up in Addis.

Makes 4 cups

4 cups water

2 tablespoons dried Ethiopian thyme leaves

1 teaspoon tea spices (see the notes on page 148)

Bring the water to a boil in a tea kettle or pot. Next add the thyme leaves and the tea spices and boil over medium heat for another 5 minutes. Remove from the heat and let stand for 2–3 minutes.

Enjoy with your favorite Ethiopian snack (pages 29–45). Some people like to add milk or cream and sugar to this.

Atmit is a traditional and popular hot beverage in Ethiopia. There are several variations on how to make it, and the two recipes I've given you here are my favorites. It is served to pregnant women and people who have a cold or an illness because of its nutritious value. After I had surgery as a child, I basically lived on atmit for a couple of weeks. I have sweet memories of my mom, my aunties, and my grandma all bringing me some daily when I was in the hospital. Each version was different. I never said whose was my favorite, but we all know it was my grandma's.

Atmit with Bula (Ethiopian Porridge Drink)
አጥሚት

Makes about 4–6 servings

2 cups bula powder

4 cups milk

2 tablespoons sugar (or honey)

½ cup kibe

In a medium pot, whisk the bula powder into the milk until smooth.

Place the pot over low heat, stir in the sugar, and cook until it is about as thick as a smoothie. Stir in the kibe and cook, stirring constantly, for another 5 minutes, just to warm through and combine the flavors.

Serve immediately.

Atmit with Gebs (Ethiopian Oats Drink)
የገብስ አጥሚት

Makes about 4–6 servings

1 cup atmit duket

2 cups water

1 tablespoon honey

½ cup milk (optional)

⅓ cup kibe (optional)

In a medium pot, whisk the atmit duket into the water until smooth.

Place the pot over low heat, stir in the honey, and cook until it is about as thick as a smoothie. (If you prefer a thinner consistency, add the milk and mix again.) Stir in the kibe (if using) and cook, stirring constantly, for another 5 minutes, just to warm through and combine the flavors.

Serve immediately.

Tej (Ethiopian Honey Wine)

ጠጅ

Tej is a popular and authentic Ethiopian drink. This delicious honey wine is served during celebrations, special events, and holidays. Served in a special glass called a *berele*, tej is a crowd favorite among Habeshas. It is sweet with some light tannins and is a wine like no other. You can store this in the fridge for up to 3 days.

Makes about 3 gallons of tej

12 cups honey

3 gallons (57 cups) water

4 ounces gesho entchet sticks

In a container large enough to hold all the liquid ingredients, minimum 5 gallons, mix together the honey and water. Cover tightly and set aside at room temperature for 3 days.

After 3 days, skim off any sediment that is floating on top, add the gesho entchet, and mix well. Cover tightly again and let sit at room temperature for a minimum of 15 days, and up to 25 days, to ferment.

After 15 days, skim off any sediment and carefully ladle only the tej liquid into a fresh container, leaving behind the gesho entchet and any sediment.

Refrigerate for at least 4 hours before serving cold alongside your favorite Ethiopian dish.

Note: Gesho entchet sticks are hops stems. You need these for a truly authentic tej.

Tella (Ethiopian Traditional Beer)

ጠላ

A popular alcoholic beverage in Ethiopia is tella: homemade beer with an earthy and hoppy flavor. We serve this at special events and on holidays and usually next to tej, as a non-sweet alternative. It takes time and requires patience, but the end result is well worth it. Note that the ingredients for this recipe are only available in Ethiopian markets. If you don't have access to an Ethiopian market, try online. You can store this in the refrigerator or at room temperature for up to 30 days.

Makes 5 gallons of tella

2 cups gesho powder

5 gallons (96 cups) water, divided

5 cups yetela kita powder

3 cups asharo powder

1 cup bekel powder

In a 6-gallon (or larger) plastic container with a lid, mix the gesho powder with 1 gallon (19 cups) of the water. Cover tightly and set aside at room temperature to ferment, 2–3 days.

Once the liquid has fermented, bake the kita. In a medium bowl, mix the yetela kita powder with 8 cups of the water. Once the mixture is thick, smooth, and lump-free, heat a mitad (see page 9) to 250°F. If you don't have a mitad, you can use a stove-top griddle over medium heat. Coat the surface of the mitad or griddle with a semi-thin layer of the batter. It should be about as thick as a layer of pancake batter. Cook until the underside is golden brown, about 5 minutes, and then flip to cook the other side until golden brown, about 5 minutes. Remove from the heat, set aside, and continue the process until all the batter has been cooked.

Once the kita is cool enough to touch, tear it into small pieces and add it to the large container of fermented liquid. Cover tightly again and let sit at room temperature for another 3 days.

Add the asharo and bekel powder to the large container and mix well. Cover tightly again and set aside at room temperature for an additional 4 days.

Next, add the remaining 3½ gallons (56 cups) of water to the large container and mix well. Make sure there is at least 10 inches between the top of the liquid and the top of the container. Cover tightly and set aside at room temperature for 2 more days to continue to ferment.

After 2 days, skim off any sediment and carefully ladle only the tela liquid into a new container, leaving behind any sediments.

Refrigerate for a minimum of 2 hours before serving cold with your favorite Ethiopian dish.

Spris (Layered Juice)
ስፕሪስ

Every time I go back home for a visit and I make my list of things to do, having this juice is at the top of my list. This layered pureed fruit smoothie drink is different from any smoothie you've ever had. I make it at least two or three times a week here in the US. The layering makes a difference, so don't skip that part. And don't be afraid to mix it up with your straw and squeeze some extra lime juice to balance out all of the flavors.

Makes 4–6 cups

½ medium ripe papayas, peeled, deseeded, and sliced

1 cup cold water, divided

4 cups ice, divided

1 cup sugar, divided

Juice of 1 lime, divided

2 medium avocados, peeled and sliced

1 large ripe mango, peeled and sliced

3 kiwis, sliced

3 strawberries, sliced

1 medium lime, cut in wedges for garnish

Place the papaya in a blender and add ¼ cup of the water, 1 cup of the ice, ¼ cup of the sugar, and 1 tablespoon of the lime juice. Blend until smooth, 3–4 minutes, and then pour into a cup and set aside.

Clean the blender and repeat the process for the avocados. Pour them into a separate cup and set aside. Repeat with the mango, pouring it into another cup. Finally, repeat with the kiwi and strawberries, pouring them into another cup.

Next layer the fruit evenly into four to six glasses, starting with the densest fruit. First, slowly spoon the papaya mixture into a glass, followed by the avocado mixture, then the mango mixture, and top it with the strawberry and kiwi mixture. It's important to spoon in the fruits rather than pouring them so you don't mix them.

Garnish with a lime wedge and enjoy with a straw and spoon.

ACKNOWLEDGMENTS

As I sat down to write a list of everyone I wanted to acknowledge, I realized how many people have been involved in my becoming the person I am today.

I would like to start by thanking God for all that He does for me and all of the blessings I have. Secondly, I would like to thank my mother, Newaye, for her wisdom, guidance, and patience, not only throughout this project but also throughout my upbringing. To my father, thank you for always making me feel like I can do anything I put my mind to and for teaching me perseverance and discipline. I hope you are looking down on me and are proud of the woman I have become.

To my brother, Nate, and sister, Lily, I have enjoyed reliving our childhood through the recipes and photos while writing this book. I am glad and thankful to have shared these experiences with you. A special thanks to Lily for pushing me to finally start this passion project that I have been talking to you about for years.

I have been blessed by so many great friendships with people that I have met on my life journey. From my dormies at LMH, to my ODU alumnus, from all the great people I had the pleasure to cook and party with in Norfolk, to all of the expats I traveled and worked with in South America, from my friends in the Bay Area to my newfound community in LA, I sure have been lucky to have met and built strong lifetime relationships with all of you. Without the shared experiences and support of each and every one of you in my life, this book would not exist.

Special thank you to my agent, Monica, my photographer, Danielle, and her team, TouchWood Editions and their team of amazing staff. I am forever grateful to all of you for believing in this project and for helping me to bring my vision to life.

Thanks to my adorable niece, Naomi, and nephew, Jeremiah, and to all my cousins, aunts, uncles, extended family members, and work colleagues. I am forever thankful for the ongoing support and love I receive every day. I am looking forward to the next chapter and adventures in this book called life.

Thank you

Ameseghinalehu

አመሰግናለሁ

With love & gratitude,

Lula

INDEX

C

D

E

F

G

H

I

L

M

N

O

P

R

S

T

V

W

Y

CONVERSION CHART

Volume

IMPERIAL	METRIC
1/8 tsp	0.5 mL
¼ tsp	1 mL
½ tsp	2.5 mL
3/4 tsp	4 mL
1 tsp	5 mL
½ Tbsp	8 mL
1 Tbsp	15 mL
1½ Tbsp	23 mL
2 Tbsp	30 mL
2½ Tbsp	38 mL
¼ cup	60 mL
1/3 cup	80 mL
½ cup	125 mL
2/3 cup	165 mL
3/4 cup	185 mL
1 cup	250 mL
1¼ cups	310 mL
1 1/3 cups	330 mL
1½ cups	375 mL
1 2/3 cups	415 mL
1¾ cups	435 mL
2 cups/ 1 pint	500 mL
2¼ cups	560 mL
2 1/3 cups	580 mL
2½ cups	625 mL
2 2/3 cups	665 mL
2¾ cups	690 mL
3 cups	750 mL
3½ cups	875 mL
4 cups	1 L
5 cups	1.25 L
6 cups	1.5 L
8 cups / 2 quarts	2 L
25 cups	6 L

Weight

IMPERIAL	METRIC
1 oz	30 g
4 oz	115 g
8 oz	225 g
10 oz	250 g
12 oz	340 g
1 lb (16 oz)	450 g

Cans

IMPERIAL	METRIC
6 oz	177 mL
10 oz	284 mL
14 oz	398 mL
16 oz	480 mL
28 oz	796 mL

Length

IMPERIAL	METRIC
1/12 inch	2 mm
1/8 inch	3 mm
1/6 inch	4 mm
¼ inch	6 mm
½ inch	12 mm
¾ inch	2 cm
1 inch	2.5 cm
1¼ inches	3 cm
1½ inches	3.5 cm
1¾ inches	4.5 cm
2 inches	5 cm
2½ inches	6.5 cm
3 inches	7.5 cm
3½ inches	9 cm
4 inches	10 cm
5 inches	12.5 cm
6 inches	15 cm
7 inches	18 cm
8 inches	20 cm
9 inches	23 cm
10 inches	25 cm
11 inches	28 cm
12 inches	30 cm
17 inches	43 cm
18 inches	46 cm
20 inches	50 cm

Temperature

(For oven temperatures, see chart below)

IMPERIAL	METRIC
115°F	46°C
150°F	66°C
160°F	71°C
170°F	77°C
180°F	82°C
185°F	85°C
190°F	88°C
200°F	93°C
240°F	116°C
247°F	119°C
250°F	121°C
290°F	143°C
300°F	149°C
350°F	177°C
360°F	182°C
370°F	188°C

Oven Temperature

IMPERIAL	METRIC
200°F	95°C
225°F	105°C
250°F	120°C
275°F	135°C
300°F	150°C
325°F	160°C
350°F	180°C
375°F	190°C
400°F	200°C
425°F	220°C
450°F	230°C

NOTES

Look what was sown by the stars

At night across the fields

I am not defined by scars

But by the incredible ability to heal

— Lemn Sissay